Abyssinia in the New Millennium

(Revised Edition)

Janetius, S.T., Mini, T.C.,

Alemayehu Tibebe

.

2016

Abyssinia in the New Millennium

(Revised Edition)

Janetius, S.T., Mini, T.C.,

Alemayehu Tibebe

2016

This book is dedicated

to all people who work for

preserving indigenous knowledge

"Indigenous people are nature's own people"

Acknowledgments

Ideas, concepts, frameworks and modules never emerge in a vacuum; it is the outcome of elaborate thinking, contemplation and philosophizing.

My intention to write this book is very simple: let the world enjoy our hard work. As I acknowledge the people behind this book, first of all I convey my sincere gratitude to my colleagues, the coauthors Dr Mini TC & Alemayehu Tibebe. It is their persistent follow-ups that pushed me forward to complete this book that was originally started few years back.

I owe a lot to my students of psychology and colleagues at the University of Gondar. It is the curiosity and radical questions of my students that helped me think beyond the conventional universalism and cultural psychology to culture-specific psychology.

I would like to express my gratitude to all those who provided support, talked things over, offered comments and assisted in the editing, proofreading and design. In a special way, I thank Shilpa (NIT Student) for helping me in the process of correction and editing.

Contents

Prologue

Ethiopia is a vast highland of rugged mountains and dissected plateaus divided by the Great Rift Valley. Traversing through those highlands and mountain folds, one encounters communities so vibrant that captures the attention of any person. It further develops and turns into a fanatic curiosity of our psyche to explore and understand more. This inquisitiveness turns into a deep regard and appreciation for the culture as one realizes that it has impacted so much on the lives of people for centuries. This was my first impression as I visited Ethiopia few years ago.

Abyssinia, Habesha, Ethiopia or Ithiopia and, in many more names these people and country are known to the outside world and historians. Often clouded by the repeated famines and the related poverty, the dignified history that dates back to the time of Biblical Old Testament and King Solomon is not known to the non-elite population of the world.

Learning the worldview of this unique people demands a discovery as well as deeper understanding of the manifold culture and diverse customs. Only then, a valid, substantial and reasonable description can be put forward. In this book, as the readers would observe, Dr.Janetius and his colleagues analyze their experiential cultural encounters as well as the unique cultural impact on the life and living of the Ethiopian people themselves in a panoramic view and scholarly analysis. And, delving into the folds of Ethiopian culture is no easy task as it demands the authors to go through almost all facets of life in Ethiopia. It is only through practical living in the society that one can understand and appreciate the vibrancy of this ancient yet advancing to be a modern society and the authors prove that.

The book traverses through diverse topics, from lighter to deeper, from generic to serious: takeoff from local culture and customary practices and trek through aspects of higher education and plunges into indigenizing knowledge base and psychology. The authors approach these topics with a psychosocial as well as diagnostic way. As the title of the book, the authors have done a magnificent job of stitching together the various bits and pieces of research knowledge in to a wonderful compilation.

Prof. Sathyabhama Varma
Chazhoor Kovilakam
Thrissur

Preface

The name Abyssinia, or better pronounced Habessinia, derived from the Arabic word Habesch, which signifies mixture or confusion, and was given to this country by the Arabs on account of the mixed character of the people. This was subsequently Latinized into Abassia and Abassinos, and hence the name Abyssinia started to prevail. The natives called themselves Itiopyavan, and their country Itiopia, or Manghesta Itiopia, the kingdom of Ethiopia. The name "Ethiopia" derives from the Greek *ethio* meaning 'burned' and *pia* meaning 'face': the land of burned-faced peoples. Aeschylus, the great Greek playwright described Ethiopia as a 'land far off, a nation of black men'. Homer depicted Ethiopians as 'pious people favored by the gods'. Today the country is officially known as the Federal Democratic Republic of Ethiopia. The country has a population of 90 million at an annual growth rate of 2.6%, of which 83% living in rural areas.

One cannot mention Ethiopia without discussing its culture. After all, culture is the one single factor that sets apart any country and people from other countries. The stepping stones to know Ethiopian culture and people are: their coffee ceremony, the colorful Orthodox Christian religious festivals, many historical monuments, simple but distinct cuisine, the repeated Olympic feat in running and its exclusive social etiquettes which are neither purely African nor Arabian. In the words of Frances Linzee Gordon, a contemporary Scottish writer who frequented Ethiopia, "Ethiopia has ensured that its culture has remained remarkably intact, unpolluted and undiluted by outside influence. The country retains its own particular language and script, its own food and drink, its own church and saints, even its own calendar and clock. Endlessly fascinating, it defies any categorization and generalization; Ethiopia is like no other country in Africa."

There were several instances in the history when Ethiopia's prominence reached its pinnacle: Ethiopia inspired the world as one of the pioneers of early civilization, not to mention its reputation as the cradle of humanity. It has seen both fortune and adverse. There were also times when its eminence hit rock bottom; when Ethiopia unwillingly developed ill repute as well as sympathy among countries for being a land of despondency and famines. However, one can say confidently that Ethiopia has travelled the distance from the glorious ancient civilization to the present, still travelling with extra vigor to make it to the new millennium of its own (Ethiopia still follows its own ancient calendar, as well the unique 12 hour time clock) with all its pride intact. The past millennium saw Ethiopia prosper as well as decline both politically and economically. The new Ethiopian millennium that started on 12 September 2007 gives great hopes and promises and, a chance to introspect its past as an incentive to energize and move forward.

One of the greatest concerns of Ethiopian government today is modernizing its education. This volume that has grown out of many studies primarily done by Dr. Janetius and his colleagues on Ethiopian culture and education, applying a culture-specific approach, pave way for a unique distinct Ethiopian intellectual identity. This collection of papers and articles analyze the basic Ethiopian cultural, religious and educational issues, with the intention of creating awareness among scholars highlighting the compelling need for a more authentic Ethiopian Indigenous knowledge base. Dr. Janetius rightly puts it in this book, 'education becomes authentic and meaningful only when it develops scientific concepts and methods that explicate cultural aspects of various life situations and phenomena'. This integration of culture into education together with the digging of ancient treasures and wisdom and patching it up in the curriculum will lead Ethiopia as a distinctive nation in the world.

The diverse issues that this book addresses will be useful to any person who would like to know something more about Ethiopia. These chapters would be a help to people of different category, like psychologists, educators, historians, sociologists, anthropologists, philosophers, and others who are interested in knowing something about Ethiopia a little deeper, as well as any simple visitor to the country. Another great beneficiary of this book would be the Ethiopian policy makers and practitioners of public health as well as social scientists. The increasing numbers of professionals concerned with cultural psychology should find this book helpful in understanding the basic cultural, religious and educational issues which are unique to Ethiopian context. It would serve very well as a supplemental text in many areas within psychology, in social science theory and methodology, cultural studies, social policy, and philosophy.

CHAPTER ONE

Aksum the Pride of Ethiopia

The announcement came in the aircraft, "please take your seat, fasten your seatbelts, we are preparing to land in Aksum". The Foker-50 aircraft started to descend; the ground and the hilly terrain of Tigray region in the Northern part of Ethiopia became more visible. I peeped through the window like an excited toddler, looking for some glimpses, recalling the pictures I saw in the internet about Aksum. The aircraft lowered its altitude and flew over thatched and tin-roofed houses, a very common scene all over Ethiopia these days. My eyes were not looking for roads and thatched villages this time, which I generally cherish to see from above through the small windows of the aircraft, rather curiously looking for something different, the obelisks which I had already pictured in my mind, as the symbol of Aksum.

A bumpy, but not scary touchdown and, at last, I landed in the Holy City of Aksum (Axum)...

I am excited... why?

I have been to many places around the world; I am already in my middle adulthood; what made me so excited about Aksum, bringing out the child within. I did not realize that I will be more excited in the following days, staying and wandering in the streets of the ancient city of Abyssinian Kings and Queens.

Aksum is about 1000 km north of Addis Ababa, high on the plateau 7200 ft above sea level. It is the holiest city of Ethiopian Orthodox Christianity with the history dating back to the time of King Solomon. Based on the Biblical stories, Queen of Sheba, who visited King Solomon in search of wisdom, was an Abyssinian Queen named Makeda and the capital of her kingdom was Aksum. According to the legends, her tomb is in Aksum and the ruins of her palace are the centre of archaeological investigation these days. Of course, there are controversies regarding the Queen of Sheba's Palace in Aksum (some archaeological investigations suggest that the ruins are 1500 rather than 2500 years old as claimed by the traditions) I am not interested in controversies because visiting the remnants of the Aksumite kingdom was pure excitement for me. However, let me remind you, Yemen also has a palace of Queen of Sheba??... UAE also has a palace of Queen Sheba???!!! In the Emirates of Ras Al Khaimah, in Shimal, archaeological excavations have unearthed a burial ground and an ancient fortress locally known as the "Palace of the Queen of Sheba". Although the actual location of the Queen of Sheba's kingdom is still a matter of dispute, many scholars believe that it spread from Northern Africa to Arabian Peninsula, covering Yemen.

Legends and fables of the Queen of Sheba are popular in Islamic, Christian, Jewish traditions and literatures. Therefore historians and scholars are not confused by different palaces in the name of Queen of Sheba as it is the practice to name important places after prominent people. Popular stories of Queen of Sheba are also wide spread throughout Arabia and Africa.

An early Abyssinian writing, Kebra Negast which means the *Book of the Glory of Kings* states that the Queen of Sheba heard about the wisdom of King Solomon and went to Jerusalem in search of wisdom. This momentous visit gave her not only wisdom and knowledge, but also a love-child from King Solomon named Menelik, who later became the first emperor of Abyssinia. According to the traditions, Menelik secretly brought the original Ark of the Covenant (known locally as *tabot*) to Abyssinia from Israel. The Ark of the Covenant, which holds the stone tables on which Moses wrote the Ten Commandments, is presumably lying in the 17th century Mary of Zion church in Aksum (if the traditional claims are true), well guarded till date by a select group of pious Orthodox monks. No one has seen the Ark of the Covenant, not allowed to verify, not even allowed entering the place, a mystery unresolved.

Aksum is the place where Christianity was declared as the 'State Religion of Abyssinia' in the 4th century by the King Ezana. The much acclaimed land mark structures of Aksum, the distinctive admirable stone architectures in Aksum are attributed to this period. By the initiative of this king, a monk *Frumentius* was consecrated in Alexandria to be the first Bishop of Ethiopia. Towards the end of the 5th century, more monks arrived either from Syria or Egypt that paved way for the inimitable crude monasticism in Ethiopia. This ancient monastic tradition still remains the cornerstone of Ethiopian Orthodox Christianity, and it is ingrained well into the culture and psyche of many Ethiopians.

Another historical significance of Aksum is the ancient *stele* or obelisks which are huge, carved pillars made of monolithic blocks of granite rocks. It is one of these obelisks that was stolen in 1937 by Italian dictator Benito Mussolini and was returned back in three pieces by the Italian government in April 2005 after lots of cry and begging from poor Ethiopians and unsuccessful requests (dating back to 1947) by the impotent United Nations Council.

In its glorious past, Abyssinian kingdom and the Aksum Dynasty's glory went beyond the Red Sea, spreading its wings in the Middle East. In the late BCs and early AD, Aksum had expanded its reputation by trading through the Red Sea to Rome and Oriental countries-as far as India and Ceylon. The *Aksumite* Kingdom flourished until the 6th century AD with its own gold and ivory trading, having its own unique language *Ge'ez* (now half-dead and coffined to the walls of the Ethiopian Orthodox Christianity), its own coins, precious stones, pottery and stone monuments and distinctive architecture.

Today, Aksum is a sleepy village (vibrant during tourist seasons – September to January, and Orthodox Christian festive seasons) near the base of the Adwa Mountains, is ruined and stands in the midst of few remarkable stone structures here and there. Some slow and steady excavations by archaeologists are going on these days under the auspicious patronage of UNESCO World Heritage Site. Archaeological excavations were first undertaken by Littman in 1906, and later by the British Institute in Eastern Africa in the 1970s. Am I wrong in being excited about Aksum?

As I entered the airport, I was welcomed by many tour guides, both official and unofficial ones, who were waiting to get one or two tourists to their hotels. As it was February, not a tourist season, it was not hard for me to bargain a room for just over 100 *Birr* per day. The name of the hotel was an interesting one '*Exodus*'. The second book of Bible did not come to my mind when I heard the name of the hotel. I just remembered Bob Marley and his song *Exodus* when I heard the name. I still wonder whether the owner of the hotel named it after the popular song of Bob Marley (Ethiopians are fond of Bob and the owner may be a fan of Jamaican Reggae King) or gave the name to signify the importance of Aksum city to its Biblical connection and the Exodus event in the Old Testament. I did not make any research further on this topic.

As the cab proceeded towards the hotel, I looked right and left, surveyed the landscape, and admired the agricultural land and stone houses here and there. A difference in the construction of houses caught my attention as I am familiar with the stick and mud houses around Gondar and other southern parts of Ethiopia; here, I saw stone houses, many of them double storied with an ancient look and structure. Beyond the farm land and stone houses of past and present, I was delighted to see a small church-like structure on the top of a hill. The hilltop had nothing except this structure. What could it be? Before I could think any further or inquire about it to the hotel boy in the cab, I saw a board '*Way to Pentalewon Monastery*'. By the time my brain took a picture and started to process the image and data of the hilltop monastery, the cab stopped at the hotel.

I was doubly happy to have the view of '*Pentalewon Monastery*' from the window of my room in the hotel. As the tradition goes, *Abba Pentalewon*, one of the Nine Saints who fled to Ethiopia to escape persecution after the Councils of Ephesus and Chalcedon proclaimed Monophysitism (a heresy) lived there. I was extremely happy to see the view of the monastery and it was my first souvenir of Aksum. There was nothing exciting to see inside the monastery, except some fine, illuminated manuscripts, metal crosses and religious articles and a *sistra* (a small musical instrument). One should appreciate the aesthetic sense of the ancient monks in selecting locations to build monasteries.

In the evening, I took a walk in the city in search of obelisks. I walked around the city looking for the skyscraper and finally reached a garden-like place near a colossal Church littered with massive teetering stone pillars of various sizes and designs. This obelisk garden also has some ruined palace-like structure, some underground tomb-like constructions and some ancient inscriptions here and there. The adjoining building has a small museum that has some good ancient collections. Undoubtedly it is one of Ethiopia's spectacular ancient sites, and no wonder UNESCO declared it as a World Heritage site.

The magnificent obelisks by no doubt represent a highly decorated lifestyle of glorious Abyssinia, far away from the present day Ethiopia, tainted by poverty and epidemics. The obelisk park is filled with numerous stone structures in various sizes and styles. Some are finely carved with decorated windows and timber-beams resembling multistoried tower-houses. Some are plain granite slabs. The largest obelisk in the garden is a broken one, lying on the ground which is said to be 35 meters long. The undamaged obelisk that stands to tell the fame of Abyssinia is more than 20-metres high. During my visit, I could see lot of maintenance work going on in the obelisk park to straighten some of the leaning obelisks and also bring back the park from its ruined state to a glorious historical site. Also important to note is that a massive obelisk that was looted by Italian fascist Mussolini was also lying under some make-shift shelter, which returned to Ethiopia after 68 years. Probably it must be standing now, as the work was progressing when I visited the place few years ago. This obelisk was taken as booty by the Italians in 1937 and was placed in Rome Piazza di Porta, near the Colosseum, despite a UN agreement to return. This stolen obelisk came back to Ethiopia in 2005, in three pieces, in an *Antonov 124* cargo plane with the estimated cost of 6 million Euros. Some plain undecorated obelisks are also seen in a field outside the present day Aksum city, opposite to the historical palace of Queen of Sheba.

A small tank named as the Queen of Sheba Bath is seen a few kilometers north of Aksum on the way to the ruined tombs of Kings. I wonder whether it has any reference to the historical Queen of Sheba or is just named after her. The tank is still used by people to collect rain water for domestic use.

Coming to the historical palace of Queen Sheba, what we see is a massive stone structure completely ruined and only a few feet of stone structures from the ground stand to tell the tale. Some archaeological excavations are going on. The historicity of the palace of Queen of Sheba is a debated topic. However, the place in Aksum which represents the historical palace of the queen is worth seeing.

Another important historical place is the Church of Mary. It is a modern church in a typical Ethiopian Orthodox style. It is said to have the Old Testament *Ark of the Covenant* guarded day and night by some monks. The funniest thing I experienced was the demand of the priests for a ticket of 100 *Birr* for foreigners just to enter the Church. I requested the priest that I want to pray in the church for which the priest asked me to pay 100 *Birr*, a shameful thing in my perception. Now, regarding the *Ark of the Covenant*, except Ethiopians no other scholars in the world would believe that the Ark is in the building adjacent to the church.

One more major historical site at Aksum is *Kaleb's* palace or tomb. It is a pair of ruined structures outside the city in a hilly area which is worth seeing. It is a massive stone structure with some underground constructions. Wonderful to see and admire the ancient kingdom that was reigning this part of the world. The stone structures are still being examined by archaeologists and no conclusive answers have been derived so far regarding the place. Thus, my expedition to the Holy City of Aksum became a remarkable event in my life and still remains one of my highly cherished memories of life.

CHAPTER TWO

Ethiopian Coffee Ceremony

Ethiopia is said to be the birth place of coffee, locally called *bunna*. Coffee is cultivated all over Ethiopia, especially in the highlands and in the southern lush forests. In the south of Addis Ababa, especially after *Shashamane* (the famous place for Bob Marley and his Rastafarians), we can see coffee plants grow natively in the lush surrounding forests, anywhere and everywhere. Unfortunately, these days coffee plantation has been replaced by a stimulant plant called *Khat* (exported to Middle East). The tender leaves of *Khat* plant when chewed causes excitement, loss of appetite and euphoria; it also increases the power of concentration and therefore commonly used by students during exam times.

Coming back to the Abyssinian coffee story, there are thousands of legends and fables about the invention of coffee in Ethiopia. The popular story goes like this: a young shepherd noticed that his goats pranced in an unusually frisky manner after chewing the bright red berries from a tree. The amused shepherd also ate a few of them and was excited after that. An orthodox monk from a monastery, who found the boy in that invigorated state enquired about the red coffee berries, ate a few of them and was awake during the midnight chanting. Thus, coffee came to the knowledge of the world. Today, more than seventy countries grow coffee and one of the most traded agricultural commodities in the world.

One of the most popular ways of welcoming a guest in Ethiopian houses is with a coffee ceremony. For anything and everything, Ethiopians organize a coffee ceremony. The coffee ceremony goes this way. It is prepared inside the house. A special kind of grass (*goozguaz*) is spread over the ground, a charcoal stove is kept and coffee beans are fried in a traditional clay fry-pan (*mitad*). Now this *mitad* is replaced in homes by a tin or metal fry-pan. Frankincense is also lit to fill the home with a sweet fragrance. When the beans are fried, the aroma of coffee spreads the air, the lady (generally coffee ceremony is done by a lady, men are not allowed to do this kind of work, no place for women emancipation) who fries the beans will take the fry-pan around the guests to spread the aroma of coffee.

Once roasting is over, it is pounded in a small traditional wooden machine (*mukecha*) then and there, meanwhile water is boiled in a mud pot (*jebena*) specially designed for this purpose and coffee powder is added in the water, allowed to boil and thus brewed. Often coffee is taken with plenty of sugar and no milk added in coffee ceremonies. It is always served in small/tiny cups (I have no idea about traditional cups, but everywhere china-clay cups are used). I always ask for coffee with less sugar so that I can enjoy the taste of coffee not sugar. Coffee ceremony is a kind of three-course drink that is taken three times - *Abol* (the first round), *Tona* (second round) and *Baraka* (third round).

By the way, do you know what is the world's most expensive coffee? *Kopi Luwak* or Civet coffee is the world's most expensive coffee. The coffee berry is eaten by the Civet (a cat like animal) and similar animals, the beans pass through their system undigested. The excreted kernel are washed, and given a light roast and wonderful delicious coffee is made. It is expensive; a cup of coffee costs around 20 to 25 Dollars.

CHPATER THREE

Culture and Human Development

The word culture would mean the entire range of activities, beliefs, lifestyle, habits, rituals, arts, ethics and behavioral patterns of a society. Yet despite the wide definition of culture, the elements of culture being too varied and divergent, this chapter on culture and developmental psychological processes will try to show explain human development from a cultural point of view. Human development is a complex interplay between the growing person and the influencing cultural environment. A lot more need to be done to use unique cultural traditions of Ethiopia as the source of scientific knowledge in the developing field called cultural psychology.

Two major processes that underlie every developmental change are maturation and learning. Maturation is the biological unfolding based on genetic makeup of the person often transmitted through heredity. Maturational changes in the brain and nervous system contribute to cognitive developments such as enhanced memory skills and increased understanding of other people's feelings and problem solving and critical thinking skills. The maturational processes guide an individual through various stages. Certain maturation seen in humans at 45 years of age cannot be seen or expected to happen at the age of 20 or 30 in the normal sense. The second major developmental process is learning through which permanent changes in thoughts, feelings, or behavior takes place mainly due to the individual's interaction with the environment. This is a life-long process by which we learn from our experiences and changes in response to the environment and social interactions. It is a complex interplay of nature and nurture or biological and sociological factors or in simple terms heredity and environment.

It is not difficult to demonstrate how human development differs from culture to culture. Just as life expectancies have differed in the course of time, human development too differs from nation to nation today. Let us look comprehensively at the unique cultural practices that influence and mould the developmental psychological process of different communities in Ethiopia.

Lifespan development: Each society has its own ways of dividing the lifespan and treating the individual who fall in to different age groups. Each society defines different status, roles privileges, and responsibilities to different age groups thus dictate what should and should not be done at different points in the life span. In Ethiopia, the Oromo community has developed its own cultural, social and political system known as the *gadaa* system. It is a unique social institution that governs the life of every individual in the society from birth to death. *Gadaa* is a way of life for Oromo people. It consists of two underlying concepts: *gadaa-sets* or ages and *gadaa-grades*. The *gadaa-sets* are the first 40 years of life through which all males pass in five eight year initiation periods. The grades are the stages through which all males enter the *gadaa* system 40 years. The grades are the stages of development through which the group passes. The full cycle of the *gadaa* consisting of 10 grades was divided in to two periods forty years each. During his life time every Oromo man had ideally to pass through 10 classes of eight years each. The *gadaa* age classification system is similar to age-sets practiced by the *Massai, kikuyu,* and *Nuer.*

	Age grades	Class (in Oromiffa)
	Birth to 8 years	debale
	8 – 16 years	kerie
	16 – 24 years	kondala
	24 – 32 years	baba
	32 – 40 years	dori
	40 – 48 years	gadda
	48 – 56 years	battu
	56 – 64 years	yubba
	64 – 72 years	yubba gadda
	72 – 80 years	jarsa

Prenatal development and birth: Prenatal development is the process of development that takes place from conception (female reproduction cell ovum is fertilized by a male reproductive cell spermatozoon) to birth through the course of approximately 280 days. During its nine months inside the womb, the fetus acquires all essential physical features and some relevant human behavior. Ethiopian women recognize their pregnancy two months after their conception, generally when they miss a couple of menstrual periods. Antenatal check up is not popular among the people. Unlike the Western societies, germinal and embryonic periods are not easily identified or cared, because most women become fully aware of the development of the fetus after the fourth month of pregnancy. At this stage, the mother would feel some kind of movement inside her womb. This indicates motor development, however at around six months, the mother clearly recognizes the movements in the womb. From seven months to birth, the mothers understand that the fetus can respond to external stimuli. Pregnant mothers clearly understand that when they are exposed to noise and heat, the fetus will make a sudden movement and kick the womb and therefore care should be taken.

Labor: Traditionally, when the mother feels that the delivery time is approaching, the pregnant woman normally goes to the house of her mother. There are certain traditions and ceremonies attached to this. When the pregnant lady arrives at her mother's village, all the men leave the family hut and the women of the village gather to provide support and encouragement. The elderly women and those who have already given birth comfort the expectant mother in all possible ways. Most women go into labor without any fear as they have already witnessed their cousins, sisters or even their own mother's labor pain. The women of the village stay with the expectant mother throughout her labor, with one woman always near her head and one behind her to support her and hold her up. Local midwife (*awaladje*) is often invited to supervise and assist the delivery. She brings her only tools mainly consist of a razor blade, some strings and the leaves of castor bean plant. The women of the family and neighborhood sing and tell stories and stay with the birthing woman as long as the labor lasts. Children come in and out of the hut but no male child over the age of seven is allowed to enter inside the house. People have their own distinctive beliefs and rituals about childbirth. *Miriam* (Virgin Mary, mother of Jesus) or is the protector during child birth. When a pregnant woman prays for safe delivery of the baby, she prays to Miriam. The castor bean leaf used in labor is also connected to Miriam[1]. As the labor progresses and the pain become more severe, women of the village pray and chant hymns to Miriam for help. If the labor is very long and difficult, the women of the village do this ritual: they carry huge rocks on their shoulders and walk around the hut with the belief of sharing some of the burden of the mother's pain and to encourage her. If the labor becomes more severe, the husband unties his belt and leaves home. When the baby arrives the birth attendant will catch the baby in the castor bean leaves. She will measure four fingers width on the umbilical cord and tie a string on both sides and use the razor blade to cut it. Another castor bean leaf is placed in the genitals and is pushed in to protect the uterus from falling out. The women dig a hole in the floor of the hut and the new mother squats and leaves the placenta in the hole where it will be buried. If the woman's perineum tears, the *awaladge* (midwife) will wash the area with warm water and paint the place with butter every day for couple of weeks.

The postpartum period: The postpartum period lasts around 40 days for Ethiopian women. The new mother stays in the hut, mostly in bed. She is considered unclean and cannot enter a church during that period. She will not cook any food or perform

---

[1] According to some unknown traditions, Miriam I(Mary, the mother of Jesus) was believed to have used the leaves of the castor bean to cover herself when she gave birth in the manger.

any of her normal duties in the house. Her mother or another woman of the village will prepare a special dish for her which is believed to have healing properties for a postpartum woman. A common dish prepared for the mother would be porridge made of roasted and crushed barley topped with spiced homemade butter; also given diluted *tella* (local beer). After the birth, the mother will not be left alone with her newborn baby for ten days. Ethiopians believe that during this period the new mother is more likely to become crazy or possessed by evil spirits and may hurt herself or the baby. To prevent this, another woman or a child will always be with her. A priest from the nearby church is invited to bless the baby and the priest sprinkles holy water on all members who have touched the woman. The possibility of death for mother or baby during childbirth is a concern for every family. If the mother dies during childbirth, the baby will be forced to swallow fresh butter until another family member can breastfeed the baby. If the family has no lactating women, the *awaladge* will see to it that one of the women of the village will agree to feed the baby.

Unique cultural practices: Pregnancy and childbearing are highly influenced by the cultural practices and customs of the society. Different cultures have different perceptions regarding pregnancy and child birth and therefore traditional customs and practices differ significantly. For instance in Ethiopia, the rituals and celebrations related to prenatal period are mainly focused on fertility, conception, cravings of pregnant mother towards food and objects, child birth, predetermining or knowing the sex of unborn child. Based on the belief system and worldview, pregnant women are also expected to avoid certain contacts and situations.

In many areas of Ethiopia when a woman is aware of her pregnancy for the first time, special coffee ceremony is hosted and when the child is delivered, the woman's mother or close relatives prepare a porridge and celebrate the birth.

In *Amhara, Tigray* and *Oromia* regions of Ethiopia, there is a belief that pregnant mothers must keep away from evil things and ugly people, because, the society expects that if she come across such things, the baby will born with the same behavior as the evil things or ugly people. It is common to massage the pregnant mother's stomach by using a stone which is smooth. Eight to nine month pregnant mothers are advised to work heavy activities in hoping to make the labor flexible and faster. Also, it is advisable to make sex around 8 and 9 months of pregnancy in order to make the child's age smart ,bright and clear locally known as *'yayin Megelecha'.*

Infancy: It is clear that infancy (birth to age one) is one of the most critical periods of the life span as the infant acquires various capacities which have a greater importance to develop new capacities and masteries in the coming stages of development. As indicated above, developmental process during infancy is also inevitably subjected to cultural influences and the author would like to discuss the unique cultural practices and customs that influence developmental processes during infancy in Ethiopia.

Infant development is characterized by rapid physical development with which the infant acquires all the necessary capacities that helps him/her to survive. The weight of the new born infant has a clinical importance to know and predict the health status of the newborn baby. In rural Ethiopia, people make judgments about the weight of the infant with no employment of modern weighting material; they simply look at a child and say the infant is big or small.

Height is measured traditionally by hand or other local materials and this measurement helps them to predict the infant physique as an adult. The milk teeth, locally known as *gig teeth* has to be extracted to avoid symptoms of diarrhea, crying and high body temperature. The early onset of milk teeth has its own connotation that it is related with hereditary matters or the deeds of the father. The society calls the father of a baby who shows early onset of milk teeth 'thief of sticks' or *yebetir leba.*

A reflex is an unlearned and involuntary response to a stimulus, readily observed in all normal newborns. However, it is obvious that there is a difference in achievement of particular motor milestone. It is complex to discuss the motor development of this period due to the lack of detailed scientific evidences. Interestingly, many Ethiopians believed that reflex actions demonstrate that the child is healthy and playing with angels. When the baby reaches six months old, the baby lays naked on many layers of round *injera* (the favorite pancake like Ethiopian food made from a tiny indigenous grain called *teff*). Everyone who are gathered for the ceremony pray and say *Thank God* that the baby is alive and physically growing. The ceremony is symbolical that the family is blessed with sufficient food to grow the baby physically healthy and show their gratitude to God. *Injera* is used because 'this is the food that keeps the people alive'. This ceremony can be organized at any time but generally after six months.

	Western		Ethiopian	
Stage	Age in month	Activities	Age	Activities
Early reflex	0–1	Reliance on inborn reflexes to know the environment; Assimilation of all experience to reflex.	0–3	Infant's reliance on reflex to know the environment. E.g.: Sucking, smiling & crying
Primary circular reactions	1–4	The infant repeated actions focusing on his own body. Accommodation modification reflex to fit new object.	3–6	The infant focus reaped actions on his own body. –assimilation appear here E.g.: Sucks his finger & things using the knowledge of breast feeding
Secondary circular reaction	4–8	Repeated actions focusing on objects /environments early sign of object permanence.	6–9	Repeated actions focusing on objects/ environment. Accommodation & imitations appear
Combined circular reaction	8–12	Deliberate combination previous required action (scheme) early sign of sense of time.	9–12	Some deliberate combination of previously acquired actions E.g.: Try to get toy by moving towards it

Another unique cultural practice during the period of infancy is *akamash* – after the successful completion of birth process, the new born infant given to the mother with a motto "hold your infant, forget the labor". The practice of *akamash* takes place followed by the handing over ceremony; it is the process of forcing the baby to swallow butter and putting butter on the infant's head to make the infant brave and a hard worker. During the ceremony conducted for male infants, a man stand with a gun at the back yard. In case of female infants, a woman stands at the backyard by holding *wesfe* (needle like material). It is believed that the infant acquires the personality of a person who performs the *akamash* practice. Contrary to the *akamash* practice, in Ethiopian Somalia region, there is a belief that the infant personality is shaped by the person who holds the infant for the first time. The majority of girls undergo some form of female genital mutilation (FGM), which is widely condemned by international health experts as damaging to both physical and psychological health. Clitoridectomies typically are performed seven days after birth and consist of an excision of the labia. A male infant also circumcised by their seventh day of infancy, the ceremony is called *Gulban day,* in this ceremony ten *Injeras* will be prepared to be eaten by young boys gathered around the ceremony.

Yet another interesting and unique practice during infancy is the process of forecasting the behavior of a child based on the season in which the child is born. This practice is prevalent around the eastern *Gojjam* areas of Ethiopia. Table above (table 3) shows season of the child birth as a predictor of behavior.

Season	Future behavior
September–November (Autumn)	Happy , Enjoyable , Romantic and sociable, because, after 3 months of rain the sun begin to rise and the flowers are seen.
December–February (Winter)	Rich since the season is harvesting time in Ethiopia
March–May (Spring)	*Egre lemlem* (lucky)
June–August (Summer)	Selfish Argumentative Aggressive easily irritated

Childhood: From age two until puberty, children gain about two to three inches in height and five to six pounds in weight every year (National Centre for Health statistics, 2000a). Infants and toddlers are quite capable of controlling their movements in relation to a stationary world, but children master the ability to move capably in a changing environment (Sayer & Gallagher, 2001). Older children have quicker reactions than young children do. In studies of reaction time, a stimulus, such as light, suddenly appears, the subject's task is to respond to it as quickly as possible – for example by pushing a button. These studies reveal that reaction time improves steadily throughout child hood (Eaton & Ritchot, 1995; Yan et al., 2000). As children get older, they can carry out any number of cognitive processes more quickly as well (Kali, 1991; Van Galen, 1993).

Contextual and systems theories hold that changes over the lifespan arise from the ongoing interactions and mutual influence between a changing organism and a changing world. Changes in the person produce changes in his or her environment; changes in the environment produce changes in the person. It is impossible to think about the individual in isolation from the physical and social contexts with which he or she interacts because they are all part of a larger system (Wachs, 2000). Therefore, it very crucial to view the childhood development with related cultural practices, norms and traditions of people. Below we will take a brief look at on the unique cultural practices, customs and traditions that produce changes in the developing child by keeping view of the Ethiopian context. Child mortality is high and they are vulnerable to different hazards resulting from stereotyped cultures and traditions and poverty. Children face different hazards for their development caused from heredity and environmental factors. Among these, the most common are the following:

- *Physical hazards* - mortality, illness, physical defects, malnutrition accidents

- *Language hazards* - difficulties in comprehension, delayed speech, speech disorder (stuttering, slurring, cluttering).

- *Emotional hazards* - emotional deprivation to much affection, dominance unpleasant emotion, heightened emotionality, failure to learn impulse control.

- *Family relationship and social hazards* - Deterioration in family relationship, change of family pattern, prejudice, antisocial behavior

- *Play hazards* - too much play time, inappropriate play equipments and surrounding.

In rural Ethiopia, children receive parental guidance very little until about age five to seven, but thereafter are socialized with authoritarian discipline. It is observed that children in these age try to experiment whatever they like to do but in response parenting is mostly punishment (different forms of laughing, physical punishment).

Boys herd cattle and girls assist their mothers in watching babies and gathering wood. According to Abbink (1996), up to age eight, *Surma* boys and girls learn and do similar things, and then it differs due to gender. Up to twelve they stay at home, later they start doing work outside. Parent-child relations are relaxed, not authoritarian. There is no corporal punishment, only verbal scolding and instructing. Children are encouraged to be verbally articulate – anticipate the actions and plans of others. *Surma* children thus develop a high 'social intelligence'. Traditionally, in the rural villages, children are given food after the elders have eaten. There was a common practice known as *kuraz* in which the elder child has to hold a lamp while father is dinning. However, modern day traditions are changing.

Unlike the *Surma* people, the child-rearing practices of *Siltigna* speaking community are more of dictatorial training often formal, authoritative, restrictive and do not encourage independence or initiative in the young. Some studies show that both parents and children in the *Silte* community are comfortable in their parent-child relationships even though it is intimidating at times. Children are not encouraged to ask questions, express their views or make conversation with adults. Early marriage is common and it is arranged by parents (Abraham, 1996).

- *Hamachisa* (Oromo) - Cultural celebration of assigning the name for the child between 2-3 years old.
- *Annaangaala* (Oromo) - Child drinks only camel milk until 6 years to be very strong
- *Ayine Tila* (Amhara) - Seven lemon and three eggs mixed together which put on the head of the child for three days by the *debatera* (local priest) to avoid diseases.

Many societies in Ethiopia have their own way of protecting children from evil things due to the popular belief that health is a 'gift of God' and evil forces can cause sickness (Janetius, 2007). Many Ethiopians believe that they need religion and the magical healing practices associated with it desperately to keep them healthy. Due to this worldview, Orthodox Christianity has many religiomagical healing practices which are very popular among every Ethiopian. The primary form of well-accepted traditional religiomagical healing for every Orthodox Christian is the Holy water or *tsebel*. Outside the church, it is the *debteras* (defrocked priests or priest students) who control the religiomagical healings. *Debteras* participate in liturgy as singers and musicians and, outside the church religiomagical healers. Sometimes they perform as herbalists, astrologers, fortune-tellers etc. *Kitab* or amulets are also prepared and given by them to be worn to wade away the evil spirits and evil eye *(buda)* from children.

Tigrian people have a harmful health practice to protect their children from evil eye *(buda)*. They do branding, burn the child's head at the corner of the eye using hot materials. They believe that when they brand the child, the pain is transmitted to the person who harms the child by his evil eye and the child is relieved form the problem.

Adolescence: Socialization generally refers to the process in which people learn the skills, knowledge, values, motives, and roles (i.e., culture) of the groups to which they belong or the communities in which they live. It should be pointed out that socialization includes two components (Long & Hadden 1985). The first component of socialization is the process, mentioned above, that leads to the adoption of culture. The second component is the outcome of the process, for example, "was the socialization successful?" or "he has been socialized to believe God exists." Socialization is seen as society's principal mechanism for influencing the development of character and behavior. Most sociologists believe that socialization is the cornerstone, both for the maintenance of society as well as well-being of the individual (Long & Hadden, 1985). Again the author would like to remind that like other stages of developmental process, adolescence is also influenced by the broader social contexts in which it occurs.

Surma people have unique adolescent cultural practice. *Surma* tribe is from the South Omo river zone in south Ethiopia bordering Sudan. The *Mursi, Suri* and *Me'en* tribes are sometimes grouped together and call the *Surma* tribe and they speak a *Nilo-Saharan* language. They are a closely-knit society with a amazing amount of commonality and cultural unity. Young men are considered warriors and they are responsible for herding stock and defending the tribe (Abbink, 1996). The distinguishing mark of

Mursi tribe is the characteristic lip plates worn by *Mursi* adolescent girls. Another significant ritual of the community is the stick fighting ceremony of adolescents which is called the '*donga*'. This ritual is performed by boys and winners are selected by *Mursi* girls to have relations.

The *Hamar* people from Omo Valley in southern Ethiopia practice bull-jumping ceremony. Naked young men try to jump over bulls without falling and once successfully complete the feat, they become member of the adult males (m*aza*). The sister of the young man performing bull-jumping will be whipping her unclothed backs even at the extent of causing wounds, probably a prayer-ritual, for the successful completion of bull jumping by her brother. The sister who takes part in this ritual will be rewarded by the brother in times of necessity. The young boy who completes the feat will be permitted to marry a girl. In addition to the unique cultural practices related with adolescence, child marriages are still practiced in rural Amhara and Tigray regions of Ethiopia. Girls normally marry at the age of twelve to fourteen and the groom three to five years older. Most marriages are arranged by the families, with a public ceremony. A priest may be invited to witness the function. There is also another form of marriage by oral consent in which the woman is paid a maid's wages and she is not eligible for any inheritance. However, the children born out of the marriage are legal and qualify for inheritance.

Adulthood: Infancy, childhood, and adolescence are preparation period for entering into adult life (Sigelman & Rider, 2003).

Physiologically, young adults are at their peak in strength, endurance, reaction time, perceptual abilities, and sexual responsiveness. Early adult hood is also a period of effective cognitive functioning and middle adult hood is a period of settling. In the middle adulthood intellectual capacities remain optimal and slowly decline in the later adulthood. Adults in their 60s and 70s face physical impairment of some kind, mainly chronic diseases, poor eyesight and hearing, slower motor coordination and reduced body-mind reactions. They also face occasional memory lapses, however, can be active socially. Let us look into the primary cultural practices and traditions that influence adult development the marriage.

Gidda Oromo community is found in Gidda Kiremu district, one of the seventeen districts of east Wollega Zone. The district is located in the northern part of the east Wollega zone. This community has a traditional marriage custom which descended from earlier times (antiquities) which is called *Naqataa* (betrothal). This form marriage is mostly arranged by the parents of the bride and groom with a great deal of negotiation. Traditionally the groom's parents search for a bride for their son. Before they make any contact with the bride's parents, the groom's parents search back seven generations to make sure that the families are not related by blood. Once this has been done, the boy's parents then make contact with the girl's parents through a mediator. The mediator goes to the home of the girl's parents and asks if their daughter is ready to marry their son. The girls' parents often impose conditions and the mediator will take the message to the boy's parents, and then arrange a date for both parents to meet at a mutually convenient location. When the parents have reached an agreement, the man and woman get engaged (betrothed). The parents then set a wedding date and they meet all the wedding expenses (Gemechu & Assefa, 2006).

Sabbat marii is another most frequently practiced marriage among this society. Strictly speaking, it is a kind of forceful marriage, which is practiced in urgency. It is asking a girl for marriage without much arrangements and preparation or it is asking a girl for marriage without prior consent and other formalities. *Sabbat marii* literally means rolling or folding a *sabbataa* (a long step of cloth, which is worn by Oromos of Gidda area round their waist). This urgent marriage is named so because of the meaning that a specific time is set for a matter to fold and and it should be done right there (Gemechu & Assefa, 2006).

Hawwii is a mode of marriage characterized by some different approaches in arranging and selecting the partners. When a boy remains *qerroo* (bachelor) for several reasons either because he is not handsome or he is from a family of low social status, it is the parents who seriously work on independently to fix a mate for him. The boy has no consent or any idea about the family of the girl. Sometimes, the girl's mother is also involved in arranging *hawwii* for her daughter. She even keeps it secret even from her husband (the girl's father). This type of marriage is usually practiced by poor people because they want to have the whole affair private and with less fan-fare. (Gemechu & Assefa, 2006).

A forceful marriage that is prevalent among Oromo people is called *butii*. This happens when the boy is refused by the girl's parents to marry her daughter or rejected by the girl herself or if he is demanded too much bride wealth and other kind of gifts which the boy cannot afford. Generally in two ways this type of marriage takes place. First, it is done with the consent of the girl, second without any prior knowledge of the girl (Gemechu & Assefa, 2006).

Wierse marriage is common in the Southern Nations specifically in Wolyta. In this marriage, the wife of a deceased brother is married by the younger brother or either of the cousins so that the responsibilities that were carried out by the deceased person will be taken care of , mainly, child rearing. This marriage is also intended to avoid conflicts in division of possessions because the replaced husband will be the owner of all the possessions of the deceased person.

Seleva is another form of marriage practiced in areas of Benishangul Gumz. An early adult (mostly the late teens and early 20's) who wanted to marry a girl in this area must kill another person and cut off the penis of the dead. The penis will be used to play the drum on the wedding ceremony.

Edir is a traditional community organization in which the members assist each other during the mourning process. Members make monthly financial contributions forming the *Edir's* fund. They will be entitled to receive a certain sum of money from this fund, the rate of which varies based on how close the deceased is to the *Edir* member. The purpose for such payment is to help cover the funeral and other expenses associated with the death. In addition, female members of the *Edir* take turns to do the house work, such as preparing food for the mourning family. People from the *Edir* come to comfort the mourners. Usually, the male members take the responsibility to arrange the funeral, and erect a temporary tent to shelter guests who come to visit the mourning family. *Edir* members are required to stay with the mourning family and comfort them for three full days (seven days in Tigray).

Ethiopia has unique cultural practices right from conception till death. For the Ethiopian people every stage of development has one or another traditional custom and practice that gives meaning and purpose for human existence. Few of the development related unique practices which are identified in this chapter will inspire scholars to go deep into this field to draft culture-specific human development theories for Ethiopian people.

CHAPTER FOUR
Traditional Orthodox Healing Practices

The unique Ethiopian Orthodox Christianity spreads its roots way back to the very early centuries of the Christendom and its religious traditions go back to the time of King Solomon and the Hebrews. Today roughly half of the Ethiopian population follow this religion. 17 to 18 thousand churches, over 100 thousand gorgeously vested simple priests with a peasant's look, enormous number of monasteries, erudite as well as slapdash monks and nuns with and without affiliation to churches and monasteries, unique half-dead liturgical language *Geez*, pectoral crosses of infinite variety and every feasible design, monotonous liturgical and paraliturgical singing accompanied by joyous clapping and excited ululation of the spontaneous faithful in the background of heavy drum beating, sizzling sound of a funny looking *sistrum* and monotonous dance movements with prayer sticks (*maqwamia*) - all tell about only one thing -an awfully unique Orthodox Christianity. Today the Orthodox Christianity has stretched its wings all over Ethiopia, more in the northern parts.

In the Fourth Century, King Ezana, declared Christianity as the State Religion of Abyssinia. Towards the end of the 5th century, monks from Syria and Egypt arrived, which prepared the way for monasticism in Ethiopian Orthodox Church. This ancient monastic tradition still remains as the cornerstone of Ethiopian Orthodox Christianity. From a critical point of view, the intimidating penance and fasting has made people, down through the centuries, notoriously lazy and lethargic as the liturgical calendar demands almost 250 days of fasting that has made the people practically not to look for work and anything beyond survival. Although this practice is popular among the rural population, the urban centers have a different outlook.

From the beginning of early centuries the Patriarch of Alexandria sent Patriarchs to Ethiopian church, the practice remained active until 1955. Since then native Ethiopian Patriarch or *Abune* heads the Church. Most village churches are round or octagonal in shape with a conical grass roof, replaced with tin roofs these days, very similar to the native hut. Also, there are older and modern basilica styled churches with stain glass windows and grand circular tower and square shaped body. The walls and ceilings of famous churches are adorned with unique Ethiopian frescoes. Monastic and older churches are larger and typically rectangular. *Tabot* (the ark) is placed in the centre of the Church just like tabernacles in the Catholic Churches; *Tabot* is carried out of the church for festivals, a typical Jewish tradition followed even today. The Ethiopian Orthodox Church also maintains many more Jewish practices like male circumcision, the Sabbath observance together with Sunday, priests sacrificing a goat or a lamb for the sick etc.

Aksum is the holiest city in Ethiopian Orthodox Christianity with the history dating back to the time of King Solomon. According to the traditions, the original *Ark of the Covenant*, which holds the stone tables on which Moses wrote the Ten Commandments, is lying somewhere in the 17th-century St. Mary of Zion church in

Aksum, guarded day and night by selected monks. No one is allowed to enter the place where this *Ark of the Covenant* is. Aksum is the place where Christianity was declared the national religion in the 4th century.

Lalibela is yet another cradle of Christianity in Ethiopia, known for its numerous wonderful red rock-hewn Churches. These remarkable monuments are considered to be one of the eighth wonders of the world, proclaiming the skill and craftsmanship of the 13th century Ethiopians. Of course, there are enough legends of supernatural origin of these churches in Lalibela.

The religious practices of Ethiopian Orthodox Christianity are primarily prayer, fasting and penance. Prayer includes both personal and communal. Communal prayer is the long liturgy in *Geez* language and often the faithful are mere spectators who don't understand it fully and join occasionally for singing and clapping. Those who fast faithfully and consider themselves pure by observing the religious practices, join for communion during liturgy. The liturgical calendar is filled with small and big feasts of Mary and Saints, almost every day. Feast days are often marked by lengthy liturgical services, carrying the *tabot*, singing, dancing, and feasting. However, festivities don't run for longer periods because another fasting day will be fast approaching. Clergy, monks and nuns and the very devout people fast almost 250 days in a year (some claim 256 days) whereas the ordinary faithful is expected to fast 165 days (180 days?) per year which includes every Wednesday and Friday and month long fasting before Christmas and Easter. Only deacons and priests with some systematic theological background can explain the liturgical calendar clearly. Other priests and faithful simply follow the calendar as a routine and daily living. The current religious and pious practices of Ethiopian Orthodox religion sounds like the Russian Orthodox practices of King Tsar's times, which Leo Tolstoy narrates in his novels.

Traditional Ethiopian Healing Practices: The World Health Organization (WHO) defines traditional medicine as health practices, approaches, knowledge and beliefs incorporating plant, animal and mineral based medicines, spiritual therapies, manual techniques and exercises, applied singularly or in combination to treat, diagnose and prevent illnesses and maintain well-being (WHO, 2001). Magic, religion, health and well-being were all mixed up in the primitive societies. It is very difficult to differentiate shamanic healing from faith and herbal healings. In the tribal as well as primitive cultures, the mixture of herbal concoction together with religious rituals, rites and magic like formulas were part of every healing practice. The people believe that sickness is either caused by natural or supernatural causes and therefore the remedy invariably a mixture of herbal concoctions and other religiomagical elements. Ethiopian society is not an exception to traditional healing practices.

Traditional healing practices in Ethiopia are often mingled with Christian, Muslim and other primitive shamanic rituals. Today in Ethiopia up to 80% of the population uses traditional healing practices in one or another way (CSA, 2001). Many of these traditional healing practices are interwoven with Ethiopian

Orthodox Christianity or other religious practices. These healing practices are concerned not only with the curing of diseases but also with the protection and promotion of religious, social, physical, mental and material wellbeing. Therefore the traditional healings become very crucial in the day to day life of every Ethiopian whether literate or illiterate, poverty stricken or economically well off.

Another contributing factor that facilitates the popularity of these traditional religiomagical healings arises from the fact that the modern medicines (western medicine) and health care facilities are restricted to the cities and towns. The modern medical facilities are provided meagerly either by government or private and a vast majority of the population has no access to this. The national average physician to population ratio is 1: 33.500 and in the remote villages 1: 510425 where as the orthodox priests ratio is 1: 1006 and it is no wonder that the local population seeks traditional medicine from orthodox priests more than doctors. These traditional religious healings are available in every village or nearby, easily accessible - socially, economically and geographically. Although scholars disagree in their classification of these traditional religious healing practices in Ethiopia, from my understanding, the traditional healing practices by Orthodox Christians could be categorized into three:

i) medicine men/women and herbalists

ii) religiomagical healers, primarily the orthodox priests and secondarily *debteras* (defrocked orthodox Christian priests)

iii) *tenquay* (witch doctors), and other lower level of healers such as *weqaby* and *kalicha* in Muslim community to whom Christians go secretly because they are forbidden by Orthodox religion.

We will consider here only the second category of healing, that is, religiomagical healing practices of Orthodox Priests and *debteras,* as it is popularly practiced and encouraged by religious heads.

Healing practices of Orthodox Priests and *Debteras:* The popular belief that health is a 'gift of God' and, evil forces can cause sickness, many Ethiopians need religion and the magical healing practices associated with it desperately to keep them healthy. Also due to this worldview, the influence of orthodox Christianity has many religiomagical healing practices which are very popular. The primary form of well-accepted traditional religiomagical healing for every Orthodox Christian is the Holy water or *tsebel.* Churches and healing places are crowded with plastic cans and bottles of water, queued to be blessed by the priest and then used for drinking, washing and sprinkling for healing. Another popular healing method often closely associated with holy water and church is baptism, fasting and penance. In this way Ethiopian orthodox Christians take baptism many times. Outside the church, it is the *debteras* (defrocked priests or priest students) who control the religiomagical healings.

Debteras participate in liturgy as singers and musicians, and outside the Church as religiomagical healers by performing as herbalists, magical healers, astrologers, fortune-tellers etc. Some Ethiopian authors consider these healers as spiritual healers whereas, in my opinion, they are purely religiomagical healers. The word spiritual is misleading for the very simple reason that they do their healing practices in the name of religion; also, they perform the healing ceremonies in a ritualistic way which has nothing to do with spirituality as it is understood today.

A major theological difference in the healing practices of priests and *debteras* is that for the priests, sin vs. virtue or evil-spirit vs. God is the basis for any sickness and healings. Therefore, they prescribe prayer (*degmit*), *tsebel* baptism (washing of sins), fasting, and penance together with holy water as a remedy. For the *debteras* it is evil spirit vs. human beings; almost all the sickness are possession of evil spirits or caused by evil spirits, therefore, prayer (*degmit*) and holy water (*tsebel*) become the integral part of any ritualistic religious healing ceremony, together with some magical healing practices. *Kitab* or amulets are also prepared and give by them to be worn to wade away the evil spirits and evil eye (*buda*). On the other hand the priests use the practice of confession, fasting, penance and Church attendance as a means of healing together with some sort of advice and guidance. The soul-father, called *yenafs-abbat* is a kind of family spiritual-doctor, common in many places makes frequent visits to the home and performs services as required. As in any indigenous community around the globe, the traditional healers as well as the local people believe that the ability to heal is God-given and to be kept in maximum secret. Often the knowledge is passed orally from generation to generation and is also safeguarded by certain group of people as family prestige. This secrecy sometimes leads to the death of this art.

The indigenous traditional healing practices can continue to be useful for communitarian values and curing for different health issues for the Ethiopian people as long as the people hold similar worldview. By taking a closer look at these healing practices, certain postulates could be drawn to enhance culture-specific transpersonal psychotherapy models. It can stimulate discussions and increase the desire for the understanding and acceptance of local indigenous cultures as against the Western doctrines and therapeutic models, frameworks on mental health and therapeutic interventions in Ethiopia.

CHPATER FIVE

Warsa Cultural Practice

Ethiopia is located in north-eastern Africa. It is a rugged mountainous country with the elevation ranging from 4624 meters peak in the Simien Mountains in the north to 120 meters below sea level in the harsh salt flats of the Danakil depression in the east. Ethiopia's scenery is diverse and fabulous with forests, savannah, numerous lakes in the depression valley in the south and, hottest place on earth in the northern Afar desert region. It is landlocked and bordered by Djibouti, Eritrea, Kenya, Somalia and Sudan. Ethiopia is home to more than 80 ethnic groups and similar number of languages; the dominant religions being Ethiopian Orthodox Christianity and Islam. The main focus of this paper is the ethnic group identified as *Workie* people and a unique cultural practice called '*Warsa*'.

Workie people live in Raya Kobo, northern part of Ethiopia, in the Province of Wello, northern border of Amhara region, bordering two other regions, namely Tigray and Afar. Majority of the people in the area are Muslims, although not very strict in their religious practices. A small minority Orthodox Christians and a very small number of people without any organized religious affiliation also live here. Tribal fights for grazing land are a common phenomenon in this area.

The people have their own unique cultural identity. The use of butter in hair and dress is widespread. When they buy white clothes, before using it, they season it with butter to have a grey or blackish tone. The butter mixed female dress is called *shirato* and male upper garment *gabi*, and lower piece of clothing *gonbiso*. However, a particular cultural practice called *'warsa'* that is associated with marriage is the centre of concern here.

For *Workie* people, courtship and love-relationship starts this way: a young boy meets a girl, attracted by her beauty; in order to express love to his lady-love, the boy throws a lemon towards her. If she picks up the lemon and smells it in his sight, she sends a positive signal telling that she is willing to accept his love; if she does not bother the lemon and does not pick, smell, she sends a message that she is not interested in the offer. Once the girl accepts his love, the boy informs his parents and they send some elders to the house of the girl for marriage proposal. Girls generally do not take initiative to tell their parents and, girl's family does not initiate any marriage talks.

The parents of the girl sometimes accept the invitation to marry in the first instance but that is not the case in majority of the cases (just to show their superiority or to tell indirectly the bridegroom's people that they are not waiting for a bridegroom). Generally, the boy's family have to meet repeatedly to pursue the bride's family members. If the proposed boy has no younger brother/s, the invitation for marriage, as a rule, is denied by the girl's family. It is completely the prerogative of the girl's family to choose a spouse for their daughters.

Once the sign of acceptance is sensed, the boy's family bring gifts to the girl's house through the mediation of some elders.

Generally a sheep, some clothes and local bread are the common first gifts. Once the gifts are accepted, the elders sit for fixing a date for marriage. During the period leading to the wedding ceremony, the friends of the bride-groom go to the bride's house and help them in their farming and other major occupations.

Preparation for marriage is done in both the houses and marriage ceremony takes place in the bride's house. On the marriage day, after some ceremonies and customary rituals in the house, the groom is taken on a horse back to the girl's house with the elders, parents, relatives and friends. After the marriage ceremony, the bride comes with the groom to his house. *Once the marriage is over, the younger brothers of the bridegroom is free to have sex with the wife of their newly married brother.*

The word *warsa* means the act of sexual intercourse between the girl and her husband's younger brothers (brother-in-laws).When a brother is engaged in sexual intercourse with his brother's wife, he keeps his stick (*dulla or shimen*) outside the door of the house so that the husband understands and avoids entering the room. If the younger brothers ignore the lady and do not accept the invitation to have sex with her, she can even ask for a divorce.

Warsa could not be seen as a cultural practice to satisfy the sexual needs of the lady. The contemporary unpopular cultural practice, female genital mutilation (FGM) is very popular in these areas, which is primarily practiced to suppress the female sexual urge. Also, the elder brother of the bridegroom, who is generally married at the time of younger brother's marriage, is not allowed to have sex with his younger brother's wife.

In most ancient as well as some modern cultures, marriage is a form of legal ownership of partners, especially man's authority over the lady and this leads to the concept that adultery is a form of stealing. The Bible and the sacred books of other religions are not an exception to this idea. The Old Testament talks about women as a form of husband's property; the New Testament Pauline doctrine instructs women to be obedient to man; the Koran teaches women's inferior status in the family and society, etc. Also, the availability and accessibility of woman for husband's sexual needs and services are one of the reasons that initiated marriage as a social institution; also gave preference for monogamy over polyandry.

Even today, there are cultures where man has the authority and power to provide his wife to others. The practice of many brothers marrying one lady like *pancha pandavas* in the Indian Epic Mahabharata is also practiced today in some parts of India. However, in the *warsa* practice of *Workie* people in Raya Kobo, the marital relationship and sexual relationship in marriage has a different outlook than the rest of the world. Chastity taboo for married women is relaxed in the family as far as the younger brothers of the husband are concerned. The common jealousy seen among men in possessing the wife exclusive for his sexual needs is not observed in *warsa* culture.

In most of the ancient cultures as well as some modern cultures today, the choice of female as wife is conditioned to a greater extent by the woman's ability and capability to perform household tasks and to bear healthy children. Therefore in the ancient times, families always looked for healthy, strongly built women as compared to women with anemic physique. Of course, the concept of female beauty today is different.

In *warsa* practice, we can infer that the rationale behind the choice of men as husband is completely conditioned by the larger number of younger brothers in husband's family, who can take care of the lady even if her husband dies. A kind of physical as well as social security for women is given top priority in the choice of mate. It is for this reason, when a boy throws a lemon to show his attraction for a girl, the girl would take the lemon only if the boy has one or more younger brothers. Even if the girl chooses a boy without younger brothers, the family of the girl would never consent to such a choice.

The courtship game in this culture (the throwing of lemon, in the starting point of male-female attraction) seems to be a free choice between a boy and a girl, an individual adventure as seen widely in the western societies, but in fact it is not so. Choice of mate is a family concern, that too, the sole decision of girl's family.

When the community was reeling under famine and epidemics of different nature, when medical facilities were not available to lead a healthy living these practices might have slowly emerged to safeguard and protect women, family and children. However, in this day of modern civilization, education, women's liberation and emancipation, this cultural practice seems outdated and archaic. Although the ethnic community looked at this practice as an instrument of social security for the lady, the problems associated with the practice are many. One of the inevitable major problem we can see would be, even the lady may not know for sure whether the children are the offspring of her married husband or her step-husband, i.e., her brother-in-law. This Raya Kobo family sexual practice *warsa* cannot be labeled as group marriage or polygamy, or polyandry because the brothers of the husband do not marry her. It is a kind of recreation or satisfaction of some basic need. If any man complains that their younger brother involves sexually with his wife, often the mother consoles and defends the situation that it is with his wife that the younger brothers learn sex.

This strange custom could be an expansion of the Jewish/Biblical custom that allows a man to consort with his deceased brother's widow and raise up offspring for his brother. This *'widow-inheritance* or *bride inheritance'* is prevalent all over the world and still practiced freely in many places and cultures. However, having sexual relationship with the elder brother's wife while he is still alive, sounds different from Jewish/Biblical and other popular concepts. This *warsa* practice gives marriage and sexual intercourse a special meaning that it is not a serious expression of deep love and individual private affair between married couples, rather a family affair for binding people.

In Ethiopia, many people from other ethnic groups and cultures however do not understand correctly the meaning of the word *warsa*. Although majority of the people heard or known the word, it is often understood differently; widespread understanding would be - husband's brother or brother's wife. Today this practice is slowly vanishing due to the increased literacy and government's propaganda against sexually transmitted diseases. However in rural areas where there is illiteracy and less urban influence, it is still practiced as an accepted custom. It is the right time now for sociologists to make some serious studies on this topic before this strange/unique cultural practice disappears due to education.

Different cultures in the universe are like differently colored roses in a garden. Preference for one color of rose over another is a matter of personal choice. However, each rose has its own beauty and fragrance; so also cultures. Knowing more about unique cultures of the world make people open-minded and more humane, help people to understand each other in a better way and live amicably.

CHAPTER SIX

Midlife & Marriage

The personality of a person has different dimensions that will be uncovered at different stages of growth by different means. At one stage in life, a reflective person will know and feel that half of the life is completed and pause for a while. He will look back and forth to wonder, question, evaluate the dimensions of growth, and look for roads less travelled. Based on the reawakening of the psychosocial and sexual growth, a person will try to redefine the goals and objectives in the light of achievement. This process of adult development that occurs roughly between the ages 40 and 55 is called midlife transition.

Midlife occurs in the adult development period in which the neglected aspects of self 'come knocking at the door'. Generally people are married at this phase of life cycle and the impacts of midlife are strongly felt within marriage where in each partner is aware of their own disappointments towards their spouse. In this period of adult development, the repressed qualities unrelentingly look for expression. The ego that has been developed and defined and the anima/animus (ideal male/female self-concept) as Carl Jung points out, will awaken and desperately look for their identification with ideal self. Married people tend to show a different self than what they showed in the early period of their marriage due to developmental process. For men, the anima comes alive and active to taunt him to look for an ideal woman who in some ways resembles the unconscious notion of the feminine that he has with himself. Similarly, in women, the animus becomes active and hunts for a man who resembles her interior notion of masculinity and conceptual ideal husband (Roberts, 1998). According to Levinson (1978), eighty percent of married people in their midlife underwent a time of personal crises or reevaluation. Levinson also points out that the twenty percent of married people who never encountered the struggle in that period were in a state of denial and would pass through this transition sooner or later. Levinson believes that there is a shift toward the interior side of oneself at midlife.

The studies by Conway (1997) also show that about seventy five percent of men and women will experience a moderate to severe midlife crisis to the extreme of affecting marriages. Citing a survey in America that shows a fifty percent increase in divorce rates among those 40 to 60 age brackets, he advises the couples to swim upstream in order to hold together their marriage. Many psychologists see men going through midlife passage as vulnerable because they tend to exaggerate their incompatibilities with their partners, or pondering over their dissatisfactions with their mate choice and perhaps even feeling a renewed longing for a more authentic 'soul mate'. Without adequate emotional support and psychological understanding for these transitional feelings, many men will choose to have affairs, or else to separate or divorce; which is often followed by a period of unfulfilling sexual promiscuity.

Marital adjustment is a lifelong process, although in the early days of marriage, one has to give serious considerations to the adjustment issues. As Laswell (1982) points out, understanding the individual trait of the spouse is ongoing process in marriage, because even if two people know each other before or at the time of marriage, there is a possibility that people change during the life cycle. Marital adjustment therefore calls for maturity that accepts and understands growth and development in the spouse (Laswell, 1982). If this growth is not experienced and realized fully, death in marital relationship is inevitable.

This chapter focuses on married people in their midlife and how this adult developmental task influences the marriage among Ethiopian men and women.

How do they face the issues and problems related to their midlife development and cope with diverse developmental issues?

Specifically, the following questions are answered: Do midlife married people experience problems in their marriage? What are the effects of midlife in the life of married men and women? How do married people manage their midlife crisis?

Although the concept of midlife and its implications on married life is a widely studied topic in the West, there is hardly any study done in Ethiopia. Therefore, this pioneer study gives a glimpse of adult development to identify and understand its implication in marriage. Since the focus is on Ethiopian married midlife people, this could be used to compare and contrast married people in other parts of the world. These findings also provide critical aid to family or marriage counselors in their work with Ethiopian mid-life clients.

Religion	Orthodox	55.95%
	Muslim	23.81%
	Protestant	09.52%
	Catholic	08.34%
	Adventist	02.38%
Education	Elementary Completed	33.30%
	High School	30.70%
	Above 12th Grade	20.00%
	No Education	16.00%
Age at marriage	Below 25	
	Male	15.5%
	Female	21.5%
	Above 25	
	Male	34.5%
	Female	28.5%

- Reasons for Marriage: Social bond and relationship – 38.09%
  Fostering Children – 34.52%
  Sexual Partner – 27.38%.
- Selection of Partner: Parental Influence – 78.57%
  Free choice of couples – 21.42%

The issues of midlife among Ethiopian married people are almost similar to that of people in the other parts of the world. The married people try to think that the partner they married is not the ideal partner roughly after 6-10 years of marriage, which shows clearly that this thought comes to their mind at the onset of midlife.

As Carl Jung points out, the anima, which is the feminine part of a man's soul, causes males to have feminine traits. It is the concept of ideal woman in a man. All feminine psychological tendencies in a man's psyche that are ignored and repressed in the first half of life will come out in the midlife. Man will try to see it in a woman and the urge to see it dominates the adult life of a man. Similarly, animus is the masculine part of woman's soul. It causes the female to have male traits. It makes the women to have a blue print of ideal man. All masculine psychological tendencies in a woman's psyche that are ignored and repressed in the first half of life will come out in the midlife. Women try to see it in a man. This unconscious task is 'to force a person to develop and to bring his own being to maturity.

Although the married people are not aware of these psychological adult development issues in their marriage, it is happening silently in their marriage. Majority of the men and women choose their partner long before the onset of midlife, not giving serious considerations for this ideal partner issues, because the concept of marriage differs among people and in their early adulthood, they don't think about it. Only in midlife, this becomes a serious concern, and marriages suffer.

The concern for ideal partner also changes between men and women. Majority of men look at beauty and attractiveness in a lady as an ideal partner characteristic; whereas women look for masculine characteristics in men. Also, both men and women look for other characteristics like honesty and tolerance in their married partner. This clearly shows that midlife married men and women are more mature than young adults in their concept of marriage partners. The initial attraction in marriage, especially for Ethiopian women were economical security, educational qualifications, where as ideal partner is more of honesty and tolerant personality.

This change of initial attraction and midlife concept of ideal partner among midlife married people is also a process of individuation and personal growth and development. For Carl

Jung, individuation means becoming your own person. Human personality is filled with contrasts and conflicts. A person has good and bad tendencies, masculine and feminine tendencies; introvert and extrovert likes and dislikes, desire to please others and be independent. In midlife, people don't like to please others but try to realize our real personality and, become one's own self. We could thus translate it as 'self-realization' of Maslow.

Although Jung calls individuation an 'ineluctable psychological necessity' he also says that it is available only to individuals who are predisposed to attain a higher degree of consciousness and reflective personalities. Just as in Maslow's hierarchy of needs, some people who never think beyond basic or survival needs, Jung too sees that many average people are content with limited horizons of life that never think of or imagine about individuation. For such people, midlife or individuation is not at all an issue.

From an active life in the first part of married life, people enter into boredom, restlessness, dullness, discontent, meaninglessness, and disillusionment in their marriage. This dissatisfaction and confusion leads midlife people to crossroads and they look forward for the road less travelled. As the married people face the crossroads, the previous identity and set goals and morals will be shaken and, try to revise their sense of identity and look for new life goals and direction.

From the above findings and discussions following conclusions could be drawn:

- Mid-life is not a deliberate conscious choice that a person makes and   people are neither aware of it nor prepared to face the challenges.

• Mid-life is not a matter of the will; it is a phenomenon that produces itself.

• Mid-life is a vulnerable period in the life of married people and it makes them to evaluate their partners and the think and rethink about the kind of choice they made.

• A new phase of psychological awareness emerges among men/women at midlife.

• Married men and women at midlife shift toward their inner-self to review and reappraise the past to modify the negative elements of their marital status.

• Majority of the married people experience slight to severe crisis which hit their marriage, which further lead men/women to have affairs, or ponder about separation or divorce, followed by a period of unfulfilling sexual promiscuity.

• The ideal partner versus real partner issue is a major taunting problem in the midlife married people's life: as Carl Jung identifies anima-animus awakening takes place, although the married people are not fully aware of it.

CHAPTER SEVEN

Culture and Personality

Anthropology, psychology, and sociology are interrelated sciences that offer distinctive perspectives on the behavior of individuals and groups. These sciences focus on the culture of the people and its influence on the individual as well as group behavior and identity. The study of culture is an indisputable aid to understand human behavior as individuals as well as members of an ethnic community. The study of personality helps us to understand interpersonal and intrapersonal relationships better. Culture and personality integrates these two views and studies human behavior, personality from an anthropological point of view. Human identity, as individuals and as part of an ethnic community, is a process that starts from childhood. Young infants develop their personal identities in the context of their families, neighborhood and peers in schools. As they grow older and older, they try to create unique personal identity that helps them to explain self in relation to others in the society and culture. Thus, from birth until death, our identity, personality and other human values are shaped by our culture.

Personality comes from the Latin root *persona*, meaning theatrical *mask*. The impression we make on others or the mask we present to the world, determines how people feel about us. Personality usually refers to that which is unique about a person, the characteristics that distinguish one person from another. Thought, emotion, and behavior as such do not constitute a personality, which is, rather, the dispositions that underlie these elements. Personality implies predictability about how a person will act or react under different circumstances. Personality is a dynamic organization within the individual of the psychological systems that determine one's unique adjustment to the environment. If we analyze various definitions of personality, we can see one thing very common in the view of all psychologists. That is: personality is consistent behavior pattern. This consistent behavior pattern makes it possible for future behaviors to be predicted with a certain degree of accuracy. That is why when someone we know behaves in a manner inconsistent with his past behavior, we are surprised and say that is not like him or when one no longer respond to a situation in the way as h/she did in the past, we say that his/her personality has changed. But the fact is, *at different stages of our development, different dimensions of our personality will come out.*

Formation and development: Heredity and environment are the two major contributors of human personality. Psychologist JB Watson challenged the world by saying '*give me few children and I will make them what you want'*. On the contrary there are psychologists who argue the importance of heredity. However, it is safe to say that both interact to form personality. Most experts believe that a child's experiences in the family are crucial for personality development. How well basic needs are met in infancy, along with later patterns of child rearing can leave a permanent mark on personality. Besides these, the development of thinking process and social and cultural traditions play vital role in the formation of personality.

Anthropologists together with psychologists and sociologists, in the last century took attempts to apply Darwin's theory of evolution to every aspect of human study. This gave rise to the Western thinking that the differences between human cultures are a series of stages as part of human evolution. This led further to the mythological concept *'civilized and primitive cultures'*. Accordingly, the Western cultures were labeled as the most *'civilized'* and Native American, African, Asian and Native Australian communities were labeled *'primitive and uncultured'* (Murphy, 2007). Franz Boas was one of the leading figures to change this racist concept (Goodenough, 1996).

In the psychological realm, culture and personality was studied by Sigmund Freud, in his book *Totem and Taboo*. He applied his psychoanalysis to the fields of archaeology, anthropology, and the study of religion. This helped him to understand his patients in their historical and cultural contexts. In the latter years, this study on culture and personality was popularized by Cora DuBois, Ruth Benedict and Margaret Mead and many other anthropologists.

Culture refers to common experiences which we share with the group or clan we live, that shape the way we view the world, interact and understand the world. Culture is expressed through various ways, mainly through language, customs, history, religion, taboo and totem, symbols, arts and architecture, gender roles, relationships, literature, fine arts, food and clothing, sport and entertainment, social and family structures, rituals and celebrations, myths and superstitions etc. Inculturation is the process of cultural transmission to infants and other new members.

In the 1930s and 1940s, American Anthropological School of Thought started to study how an individual's personality is shaped by the culture. Cora DuBois in the 1930s, hypothesized that the adult personality is shaped by parenting and early childhood; how and when children are fed and weaned, the amount of love and affection they received. She conducted her research on Alor Island in Indonesia and found out that mothers resume gardening soon after the birth of their children, leaving their children with older women. In the custody and day-care of older women (grandmother or an elderly aunt) the children received little affection or attention and they were often brutally punished or teased (DuBois, 1960). This childhood experience leads to adult personalities who are hostile, suspicious, jealous and violent.

Another leading figure in the field of culture and personality is Margaret Mead. Her best-known study was on gender issues. In her book *Sex and Temperament in Three Primitive Societies* (1935), she proves that gender characteristics were not shaped by biology or genetic factors rather culture. Mead's research answers a basic question in cultural anthropology, 'why are we the way we are? By explaining the association between childrearing custom and human development, she concludes that human behavior is a by-product of culture. The cultural traits are learned and reinforced at different stages of life and development. Also, most of her conclusions are criticized, especially her studies on Samoan culture was strongly opposed by New Zealand anthropologist Derek Freeman.

Many psychologists and anthropologists who are influenced by the theory of evolution believe that gender differences are biological.

Cavemen went for hunting, cavewomen stayed near the house, rearing children and cooking food that gave distinct physical as well as psychological characteristics which are seen in our biology and personality (Helen Fisher, 1983). However, the researches by Mead give a different picture. She studied and compared three societies from the cultural point of view, specifically parenting care: Arapesh, Mundugumor and Tchambuli. In Arapesh society, both men and women had nurturing and gentle personalities, both valued parental roles and participated in child care; in Mundugumor, both men and women were assertive, aggressive and loud; in Tchambuli men were preoccupied with their looks, gossiped, did little productive work while the women fished, gardened and managed the household. She concludes, by changing culture, you could change personality (Mead, 1949).

Cultural psychologists have noted that some aspects of personality differ across cultural groups. For example, Americans and Asians have slightly different conceptions of self. American culture promotes a view of the self as independent. Americans tend to describe themselves in terms of personal attributes, values and achievements, and they learn to be self-reliant, to compete with others, and to value their uniqueness. Many Asian cultures, such as those of Japan, China and India promote a view of the self as interdependent. People from India tend to identify self-esteem as pride and often identify themselves in terms of which group they belong to. They learn to rely on others, to be modest about achievements. Similar differences can be seen in Africa also. The cultural psychology believes that culture influences aggressiveness in males. However, researches show that in places where there are plentiful resources and no serious threats to survival, such as Tahiti or Sudest Island near New Guinea, males are not socialized to be aggressive (Murphy, 2007). Culture also influences altruism. Research shows that children tend to offer support or unselfish suggestions more frequently in cultures where they are expected to help with chores such as food preparation and caring for younger siblings. Ideally, cultural psychologists acknowledge that not all members of a culture behave similarly. Variation exists within every culture, in terms of both individuals and subcultures. In this regard we can make a difference between culture-specific psychology and cross-cultural psychology. Cross-cultural psychology highlights the similarity across different cultures where as culture-specific psychology highlights the differences and uniqueness among cultures.

One of the leading psychological theories often talked in this connection is Freud's psychoanalysis about early childhood development. His theory raises the question, if all humans are hereditarily equal, why people are unique from one society to another. Freud did not give high emphasis to culture-specific human development. However, his theory of human development paves way for modern studies on human development.

If we apply the theory of Freud in Ethiopian or African context, we have to classify all the people of this part of the world as having fixations that lead to poor adult development. In Ethiopia and in most parts of Africa in general, there is a longer period of breast-feeding compared to the Western and other cultures. Another cultural and childrearing issue that hinders the application of

Freud's theory - the toilet training period: toilet training as assumed by Freud is out of context in this culture. Children go for toilet anywhere and everywhere without discretion and without parental guidance.

African Psychology Characteristics: Africa has personality style derived from its unique cultural practices. African way of thinking, behaving and other cognitive processes derive from a restrictive, closed, conservative indigenous socio-cultural conditions, and this has been contaminated by Western cultural influences. Nyasani identifies and discusses sociality, patience, tolerance, sympathy and acceptance as:

"... African mind seems to reveal itself ... through what may rightly be called a congenital trait of sociality or sociability. It further reveals itself as a virtuous natural endowment of patience and tolerance. And lastly it manifests itself as a natural disposition for mutual sympathy and acceptance. These three areas then appear to serve as important landmarks in the general description of the phenomenology of the African mind".

The study of culture and personality is a by-product of three disciplines – psychology, sociology and anthropology. We need to utilize all these three disciplines to understand the growth and development of personal or social identity and personality. Influenced by the theory of evolution, Freud's psychoanalysis and many other social-psychological theories and concepts, anthropologists began searching for common aspects that would characterize differing peoples by their cultures. In an attempt to avoid racist, hierarchical culture models, a new breed of anthropologists study culture and psychology to explain the riddles of human behavior.

.

CHAPTER EIGHT

Far from Freud:
Psychosexual Development

The definitions of health and disease, normal and abnormal are determined by the prevailing social norms and they are culturally determined. Culture refers to a group or community with whom common experiences are shared, that shape the way people interact and understand the outside world. It includes community in which we are born, gender, race, or national origin, religion etc.; also the groups and communities we join or become part of. Our culture influences how we grow, develop, think and behave, interact and participate in groups and communities.

In the field of psychology, culture is understood to pose a barrier to culture-specific understanding of human development. The Western theories of human behavior, development and personality modules that are popularized all over the world do not fit to the needs of people from another culture and do not explain fully. Therefore, an effective psychologist should work in harmony with background influences of human conditions specifically the tradition, life world, environmental and geographic condition of the specific people.

Psychologists are more and more becoming aware of the problems of cultural relativism and focus increasingly on cultural contextualization or culture-specific approach in understanding and answering human behavior and mental health issues. As a psychologist and counselor, my main difficulty in understanding human behavior in either Asia or Africa is that, almost all the theoretical frameworks used in understanding human behavior, personality, human development and counseling process are of Western origin that reflects their culture, thinking and lifeworld. In addition, many of the basic assumptions of psychology such as: the scientific and rational approach, the striving for self-actualization and the preference for active adjustment over passive acceptance reflect the socio-economic, political and philosophical context of the Western Euro-American cultures.

In fact, just like any reflecting psychologist in the East, we have reservations to the applicability of many western theories of psychology in Asia and Africa. The difficulties deepened more in the recent years as I started my work in Ethiopia. Practicing as a counseling psychologist at the University of Gondar made me realize that the psychosexual development theory of Freud is not culture-sensitive and needs a lot of modifications and revisions in order to apply in Ethiopia or African cultures. However, thinking about Freud in African culture, specifically in Ethiopian culture, force me to make a war cry for culture-specific theories of human development and personality.

Psychosexual development: According to Freud a person has two basic instincts - sex (life instinct) and aggression (death instinct)[2].The *libido* is the available energy of sex. Sexual excitation arises from erogenous zones in the human body. The change in the site of excitation underlies the moment from stage to stage

---

[2] Neo-Freudians use the term Eros & Thanatos

development. and the task is to achieve sex drive equilibrium. The other instinct is aggression (death instinct). He believed that a person has desire to come back to the original inorganic state; further, a person who tries or commits suicide satisfies his or her death instinct. The mind displays three topographic regions: the unconscious, preconscious and conscious. The unconscious is largely unknown territory, refers to thoughts and feelings that are repressed. The preconscious and, especially, the conscious have familiar terrain. The preconscious becomes conscious by forming mental images or linking up with language.

Sigmund Freud's psychosexual development can be defined as a harmonious interplay of the individual's psychological and sexual capacities within an ordered and ethical value system. A person's psychological growth is conditioned by the *libido* or the inner energy that is reflected in sexual growth. Also, our personality develops as we move through a series of psychosexual stages. Freud's most basic hypothesis was that each child is born with basic instincts, a source of basic energy called *libido* (vaguely translated as sexual pleasure). Further, each child's *libido* becomes successively focused on various parts of the body (in addition to people and objects) in the course of development. Freud was influenced by Charles Darwin's theory of evolution. Therefore, emphasizes the biological basis of human development a lot. Freud talks about four/five stages of development (latency period is not considered a stage of development by many authors). Each stage is characterized by different demands for libido gratification and ways of achieving; if any trouble arises in normal development process, fixations arise to hinder the personality all through our life. During the first postnatal year, *libido* (sexual pleasure) is initially focused on the mouth and its activities; nursing enables the infant to derive gratification through a pleasurable reduction of tension in the oral region. Infants seek gratification through mouth, mainly sucking the breast, feeding, crying, and other oral explorations. Freud called this the oral stage of development. Fixation at this stage will affect the growth of the child, especially the personality, leading to disturbed adult behaviors like being passive, overly dependent, verbal aggression, impatience, greediness, and a preoccupation with giving and taking. Adult habits like smoking, overeating, thumb sucking, objects chewing are expressions of fixations and poor oral development. During the second year, the source of excitation is said to shift to the anal area, and the start of toilet training leads the child to invest libido in the anal functions. Freud called this period of development the anal stage. Too little gratification in this stage results fixation often reflected as orderliness, neatness, rigidity, obstinate, stingy, and possessive and other compulsive behaviors.

During the period from three through six years, the child's attention is attracted to sensations from the genitals, and Freud called this stage the phallic stage. This stage is one of the important periods of psychological development. Oedipus complex occurs in male children and penis envy in females. Oedipal conflict according to Freud takes place when most male children realize the sex difference in their organs, and the male child identifies with the father and desires his mother. Castration anxiety makes the male child afraid of the father (a strange feeling according to Freud that the child fears that he may lose his sex organ for such thoughts). In the female, it is labeled as Electra complex (by the latter psychologists) where the female child desires her father and hates the mother thinking that it is the mother who created her without penis. Conflicts and fixations at this stage, according to Freud lead to homosexuality, authority problems, and rejection of appropriate gender roles.

Latency stage is the years before puberty and no significant developments take place; libido is dormant at this stage. Repressed drives at this period may lead to formation of friendships, or hobbies. Finally, the genital stage of development arrives in which mature gratification is sought in a heterosexual love relationship with another person. Freud believed that adult emotional problems result from either deprivation or excessive gratification during the oral, anal, or phallic stages.

In Ethiopia, there is a longer period of breast-feeding compared to the Western and other cultures. For example, in my research, almost all the students surveyed categorically state that they breastfeed up to 3½ to 4 years. The only exception is poverty or famine, in such case the mother has no milk and the child is deprived of longer breast feeding. Another cultural issue that hinders the application is the second stage of Freud's theory - the toilet training period. Practically there is no toilet training as such given to children in this part of the world, except few urban cities. In all other places, children go for toilet anywhere and everywhere without discretion and without parental guidance. Although there are many projects by western countries and WHO funding for public health that shows that almost majority of the population has toilet facilities, in my observation research projects of public health are only in papers not seen in the ground. If we apply the theory of Freud in this context, we have to classify all the people of Ethiopia having fixations that lead to poor adult development, which would be farce. How can one say that the whole country is suffering from neurosis because of a western theory of human development? The major problem to the application of this theory in the Ethiopian context arises in the age brackets given by Freud in table below.

Freudian Age	Ethiopian Age	Stage	Pleasure Source	Conflict/Difference
0-2	0-3.5/4	Oral	Mouth: sucking, biting, swallowing	Weaning away from mother's breast
2-4	4-6	Anal	Anus: defecating or retaining feces	Toilet training Ethiopia has no strict toilet training by parents
4-5	7-8	Phallic	Genitals	Oedipus & Electra
6-puberty	8-9	Latency		
Puberty onwards	Puberty onwards	Genital	Physical sexual changes Reawakening of repressed needs Direct sexual feeling towards others	Social rules

Throughout the world, indigenous peoples have maintained their unique philosophy, worldviews and associated knowledge systems for centuries to explain realities, which are often ignored or undermined by Western civilization and society. The indigenous peoples of Asia and Africa and their unique lifestyles are often unnoticed or under-appreciated. Realizing the value of indigenous wisdom or knowledge, uniqueness of different cultures of different continents, many scholars today try to create psychology for specific culture and population integrating the core values and beliefs, customs of different societies. The social, geographical, cultural factors play a vital role in the understanding of human growth, development, personality, maturity etc... It is evident that Western-made psychology and theories do not provide enough knowledge about people and their behavior in other parts of the world. Therefore, we need culture-specific theories of human behavior, human development and personality.

The theory of Freud clearly reflects the human development in the society he lived and similar societies around the world. Therefore, it is applicable in such societies. However, when we try to understand the human development applying the psychosexual development theory in Ethiopian context, due to cultural, environmental and social conditions of the people; it is not at all applicable to the majority of the population. So, Ethiopian psychosexual development is far from Freud.

CHAPTER NINE

Quality Teacher Characteristics[3]

---

[3] An abridged version of the paper presented at the 18th Annual Research Conference, University of Gondar, Ethiopia by Dr Janetius, Dr Mini TC & Bekele Workie

This chapter is aimed at helping educationalists in Ethiopia to prepare quality teachers through pertinent pedagogical training and renewal programs so that identified characteristics could be highlighted; For teachers to have self-awareness about current condition and expectations of students so that positive classroom can be created and quality education provided to the satisfaction of students. Success in education depends on several factors such as institutional physical and personnel environment, student's personality attributes and efforts, interaction and interpersonal relationship with teachers and peers. Research findings in the developed countries identify positive classroom environment as an influential factor in the academic outcome (Weishen & Peng, 1993; Ferguson, 1998; Hanushek, Kain, & Rivkin, 1999).

A positive classroom is that in which a teacher becomes facilitator by helping pupils to access information, encourage creative ideas and help to solve problems, thus pave way for authentic learning in a multidimensional way.

This condition expects quality teachers with adequate training and orientation, well-bred personal attributes and characteristics to create a caring and conscientious classroom relationship. These in turn produce better academic outcome reflected in students' interest in the course being taught, increased knowledge in the field, higher grades and ultimately better opportunity for success.

The current situation in many classroom environment and teacher-student interactions are seen in the form of an authoritarian teacher who claims exclusive authority over knowledge who makes students drifters looking for grade. Therefore, a quality teacher and a positive classroom conducive to bring desired outcome is essential and solicits appropriate preparation of teachers, adequate training in communication and interpersonal relationship, years of experience (Hanushek, 1986), appropriate education (Greenwald, Hedges, & Laine, 1996; Hanushek, 1986; Ferguson, 1998; Hanushek, Kain, & Rivkin, 1999) academic proficiency and competency (Strauss & Vogt, 2001; Greenwald et al. 1996) in the subject matter being taught (Goldhaber & Brewer, 1997; Monk & King-Rice, 1994) and, graduate degree-job placement convergence. If some of these qualities are satisfied and perceived by the students in a teacher, consequential education and success can be expected. To prepare quality teachers and consequential education, two questions are put forward:

(i)   What are the quality teacher characteristics?

(ii) How quality teacher characteristics have their influence on academic outcome of the students?

Ethiopian students perceive education, academics, work experience, positive relationship with students and personal attributes of the teacher the characteristics of quality teacher.

- 93.4% of the students being studied consider education as the top characteristic of a quality teacher
- Academics that is knowledge and intellectual/academic capacity (89.4%)

- Teaching and work experience (87.4%)
- Positive relationship with the students (85.2%)
- Personal characteristics, attributes, personality (80%).

Education: In the category of education of a teacher, the significant factor identified was 'educated abroad'. The other variables namely, locally educated and higher degree of the teacher – were identified as non-significant factors. This shows the higher values that the students give to teachers who are educated abroad. This also reflects on the fact that the students do not trust or value the education provided by the local Ethiopian universities, but they have high regard for foreign universities.

Academics: This refers to the knowledge and intellectual/academic capacity of the teacher. The significant factors identified by the students are: intellectual curiosity to learn/ know new things and, clear, good knowledge of subject matter and the lessons being taught. Surprisingly, cultural integration and applicability of the lesson is not considered by the students as a significant characteristic denoting quality teacher.

Teaching and work experience: The students perceive many years of teaching experience and experience in different fields other than teaching/ together with teaching as quality teacher characteristics. However, teaching experience in difference colleges is not considered a significant characteristic of a quality teacher.

Positive relationship with the students: The students do not perceive this as an important factor. However, positive relationship between student and teacher has been identified and appreciated all over the world as one of the important psychological conditions in any learning process. 'Accept students as they are' is a highly appreciated concept among students. Care and respect for students and periodical encouragement are the factors considered by the students.

Personal characteristics: The last category selected by Ethiopian students is personal characteristics, attributes, personality of the teacher. In this, the students identify self-discipline and character as well as unbiased equal treatment in dealing with students as the significant factors. The students do not expect the teacher to be exemplary to them.

- Ethiopian students show high interest in the course being taught, like to increased their knowledge in the specific field and see education as source of success in life.

- They expect in a teacher high-class education, academic intellectual curiosity and desire to learn, good work experience and positive relationship with students.

- They do not give much importance to the personal attributes to qualify a quality teacher.

- They give high regard for the education of teacher from a foreign country.

- Care and respect for students, encouragement given are very important for students to accept a teacher as a quality teacher.

CHAPTER TEN

Culture-Sensitive Teaching

The number of students enrolling in centers of higher education in Ethiopia is increasing dramatically in the last few years. In addition to the eight universities established few years ago, more universities have come into existence in this year that makes the current number of universities in the country to thirty one[4]. Moreover, private colleges are also mushrooming in every town. However, teaching in a college and sitting in a college classroom becomes a challenge today. One of the reasons for this challenging situation is that the lessons and lectures do not share the worldview of the students, do not focus on the culture of the society in which they are born and brought up.

A good educational system for sustainable development of a country must identify knowledge which is relevant to the socio-cultural condition and context. One of the disadvantages of present pedagogy is that there are differences in the classroom culture seen in teaching-learning methodology and the student's native culture, tradition and beliefs with which they are born and brought up.

Although we know that learner's culture, family background, and socioeconomic factors affect the learning and other cognitive

---

[4] 2015 April data

processes, the cultural difference they face in their education and classrooms make them struggle for academic accomplishments. Academic world in Ethiopia maintains a distance from local culture due to the western influence of education. Although Ethiopia was never colonized by any foreign forces or Ethiopian educational system is by no means a by-product of any direct colonialism, it is obvious that the incursion of foreign models of pedagogy in Ethiopian universities is very powerful. Most of the times, American, British or European models of syllabi, evaluation modalities and pedagogy are welcomed unscrupulously, rated highly, accepted blindly as apt and adequate.

The traditional teaching model followed in many colleges and universities are criticized all over the world for not being responsive to the student's specific needs and not accommodating students' interests and abilities. It also fails to reach diverse student population in the classroom and often neglect active student participation. Hillocks (1995) assert that teachers should possess specialized knowledge of students and also how to represent and teach the knowledge to them. In other words, to be effective in the classroom, a teacher needs to know the subject matter, the student population and appropriate pedagogy.

Culture-sensitive classroom is that in which the teacher compares and contrasts knowledge cross-culturally and multi-culturally, integrates materials, concepts, and values of local culture into pedagogy and imparts that knowledge in the unique learning style of the learner. Knowledge should be taught from the cultural base of the learner (Henderson, 1996). Moreover, educationalists and social scientists all over the world cry for sustainable development education.

For sustainable development education, the curriculum and classroom activities should reflect the cultural contexts of students expressed through language, religious customs, rituals and celebrations, taboo and totem, symbols of arts and architecture, literature and fine-arts, social and family structures, myths and superstitions etc. As Ladson-Billings (1994) points out, content integration (the inclusion of materials, concepts, and values of local culture) will be of great help to make education appealing and applicable to students. To answer the call for sustainable development education, culture-sensitive classroom is an ideal solution that will ensure students the opportunity to acquire knowledge, skills and values needed to make social and environmental impacts by making the classroom an interesting and enchanting place of learning.

This article evaluates the current culture-sensitiveness of the college teachers in Ethiopia by knowing how they are perceived by the students. For this purpose, data was collected from 1169 students and 53 teachers of Addis Ababa and Gondar Universities. The results from the students reveal that the average culture-sensitiveness of instructors in these universities is 41.34%. 85.4% of students were taught by Ethiopian and 14.6% foreign teachers. In the University of Gondar, 17 sessions of Brainstorming were conducted for 926 sample students from 11 departments who were taught by 53 Ethiopian and 12 foreign teachers. The instructor's culture-sensitiveness is perceived by students as 35.22%.

Conceptual Model for Culture-Sensitive Classroom

Today there is a strong awareness among educationalists to move from teacher-centered to learner-centered classroom. The current situation in the classroom is often the contrary. It is primarily verbal and out-of- learner context that makes students mere passive recipients. It is neither personally constructed for a specific population of students nor applicable in a particular context and culture of the students. The pedagogical choices teachers make are often reflection and repetition of the teacher-student interactions the teachers themselves once experienced. As against this classroom situation, McClanaghan (2000) encourages teachers to be sensitive to the subject matter, knowledge of students and their orientation and adopt appropriate pedagogy. The contemporary researches and theories of education, pedagogy and learning style amply highlight the learning differences among students of different culture (Ladson & Billings, 1995). The centre of focus in the modern pedagogy is the learner and therefore learners' style and taste must be given high priority (Smith, 2002). Embedded with commitment, the teachers should intentionally take the students to the real life situations of what is being taught and, make the students recognize the relevance of the lessons in their personal life in particular and social life in general (Janetius & Mulat, 2006). This paradigm shift calls for deeper understanding of individual and cultural differences of students and cultural understanding, integration and adaptation in imparting knowledge with students. In order to apply appropriate, effective pedagogy in universities and colleges the authors propose *Shell-Culture Adaptation Model (Shell-CAm).*

A general question that could be raised when we talk about a conceptual model for culture-sensitive classroom would be 'Why should we incorporate culture into pedagogy?' To answer this question, the authors quote the psychology of Swiss psychologist Carl Gustav Jung (1875–1961) namely archetypal psychology, which talks about human mind and its functioning. Although Carl Jung (1969) conceptualized archetypal psychology in psychotherapy and clinical scenario, one can effortlessly transfer his concepts on the basic functioning of human mind in classroom setting and teaching-learning process as well.

The archetypal patterns that are in our mind are the part of cognitive bases of humans. They are to a greater extent congenital and modified by historical and socio-cultural factors. Based upon cultural influences as well as one's own unique history, they consciously and unconsciously influence human behaviors (Adams, 2007). These archetypal patterns in human mind could be compared to a computer operating system on which the education which is the software that executes its functions.

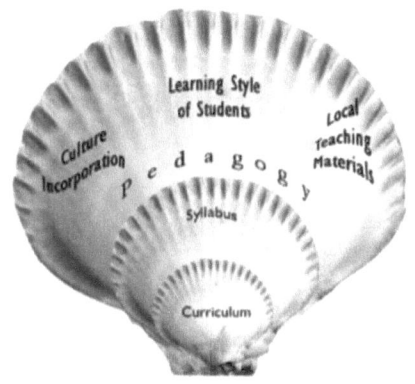

Shell-CAm is the conceptual model proposed by the authors. It is named Shell-CAm because the diagram of scallop shell is used to present the model. The scallop shell is the symbol of pilgrimage and the authors consider classroom education as a pilgrimage towards wisdom.

The primary goal of *Shell-CAm* is to help teachers adapt a new paradigm in pedagogy and the ultimate goal is to help students feel at home in the classroom, make learning more purposive and meaningful. The model has three components namely curriculum, syllabus and pedagogy. It is beyond the scope of this study to propose culture-sensitive curriculum and syllabus and therefore the model explains pedagogy that will lead to culture-sensitive classroom and teaching. The pedagogy consists of three elements:

    i) culture incorporation

    ii) learning style of students

    iii) local teaching materials

Since the main scope of the paper is a culture-sensitive classroom, the model focuses mainly on pedagogy and its three components.

1. Culture incorporation: Early life experiences and the values of a person's culture affect both the expectations and the processing of learning. Therefore, culture-incorporation is given high priority in this model, that is, moving from theories to real life issues in the classroom. By focusing and explaining theories with real life issues that reflect cultural, sociopolitical and family issues of everyday life we can easily incorporate culture. This could be done in two ways: a) by incorporating culture specific examples and application modalities to every lesson being taught, b) comparing and contrasting knowledge with cross-cultural and multi-cultural references. For example, for a lesson in sociology of religion or anthropology of religion, call an Orthodox Christian priest or a Mullah to the classroom to explain the theology of particular religion; to teach family and parenting styles in Psychology, call a parent to explain family issues; while teaching about banking, invite the manager of the Commercial Bank from the town to discuss how the system works etc.

The following practical guidelines could be considered for culture-incorporation:

- encourage learning through involvement by participatory methods like field trips
- require from the students assignments and interview reports which are contextualized
- provide cultural orientation for foreign and new teachers
- invite local expertise to the classroom to explain facts from local culture
- identify indigenous knowledge and incorporate them in classroom activities
- invite foreign expertise to compare and contrast ideas and facts with cross-cultural praxes and making aware of multi-cultural issues to the students
- encourage group discussions in the classroom.

2. Learning style: Students differ in their cognitive (perception and gaining knowledge) and conceptualizing styles (forming ideas and thinking patterns). Also, they differ in what they do with the knowledge they gain. Some students always look for connections and relations between things; others may give preference for thoughts, ideas, or facts that trigger multitude of new directions and vistas. Some may categorize ideas in a linear, sequential way, while others organize their thoughts in clusters and random patterns. Some may prefer to think spontaneously and impulsively while others deliberate and reflective. The knowledge bases of the students are reflected in the culture and learning styles and teachers need to examine their own instructional practices and make them sensitive in providing diverse learning experiences to the students.

The preferred styles of the students should be given precedence over the teaching style of the teacher himself. This calls for flexibility from the part of the teachers in their approach and classroom strategies. The following are few practical guidelines (Janetius & Mulat, 2006) for teaching in tune with the learning styles of the students:

- while presenting the course outline to the students, the teacher can request the students their preferred topics in the course outline and highlight those topics in the teaching
- encourage students to different learning activities: ask them to prepare posters, drawings, interview people, etc.
- consider multi-media presentations frequently
- observe the students' learning preferences and generate information about their strengths
- ask the students to assess their own intelligences and understand their learning preferences
- do not hesitate to consult your colleagues who are more creative to find ways and means of better classroom management

3. Locally produced resource materials: One of the important factors that drag back the present educational system is the lack of locally prepared teaching materials. Even though the ministry of education and many foreign donor institutions encourage preparation of local teaching materials, to the surprise of the authors, many teaching materials prepared locally lacks culture-specificity. For example, a research methodology book prepared as Lecture notes in one university was thoroughly scrutinized by the authors to identify factors of culture integration or culture adaptation or cross-cultural references showed zero percentage localized. It is merely a repetition of western ideas, concepts and theories compiled together. Therefore, locally prepared teaching resources should be encouraged in such a way that they reflect local culture and need of the students. The teaching learning process should not thrust the values, beliefs and behaviors of the dominant western cultures, which only need to be learned for general awareness and understanding rather than for advocated active use. Otherwise the learning process will lead to source credibility bias. Different folk art forms, folksongs, stories, riddles, and games, should be included as teaching material. The teachers should be encouraged to prepare culture specific, contextualized theories and concepts and that should take precedence over foreign made theories. For example, Sigmund Freud is one of the psychologists the world admires and his psycho-sexual development theory is highly appreciated in the psychological circles all over the world and it fills the books on human development for centuries. However, applying this theory in the African culture, specifically in Ethiopia would lead to the fallacious conclusion that all the children of Ethiopia having fixations in their early development that lead to poor adult development (Janetius, 2007). Therefore making use of locally produced resource materials like reports, videos, maps, books, local cultural documents must be given priority in every aspect. Also, educationalists and scholars of various fields should come forward to prepare contextualized theories in all the possible areas.Few practical guidelines:

- recent local research articles and data should be incorporated in the syllabi and classroom lectures
- books and materials of local authors should be incorporated as reference materials
- folklores, local proverbs and stories of local heroes could be identified and studied more for integration into education
- contextualized theories and concepts should be given preference over foreign theories
- encourage cultural festivals as a part of classroom activity.

Teaching is a cooperative, multi-dimensional tool in which the teacher and the students interact in the classroom. This is done by incorporating the culture, imparting knowledge in the preferred learning style of the learner and presenting subject matter with as many local resources as possible. This integrative, culture-sensitive classroom would be an ideal educational setting because it stimulates connections that are made naturally in students' minds and stimulates the cognitive abilities that give opportunity to grasp ideas and study topics in-depth in a very personal way.

A teacher who develops methodologies sensitive to the needs of the learners will foster success in the academic achievement of the students as well as in their professional development as teachers. Administrators and curriculum specialists and educators should therefore work hard to create awareness among teachers about the individual learning styles of the students, cultural, cross-cultural and multi-cultural application of lessons and give priority to local resource materials. If this is done in the classrooms, the teachers can transform the dormant education into a pilgrimage of wisdom, convert classroom into a temple of learning that will produce genuine scholars and original thinkers for a sustainable development of the country.

CHAPTER ELEVEN

Indigenizing Knowledge Base

Culture is in limelight today and its distinctiveness is understood in every sphere of education. Culture refers to a group or community with whom we share common experiences that shape the way we interact and understand the world. Culture is expressed through language, customs, history, religion, taboo and totem, symbols, arts and architecture, gender roles, relationships, literature, fine-arts, food and clothing, sport and entertainment, social and family structures, rituals and celebrations, myths and superstitions. The UN declaration of the Rights of Indigenous Peoples (2007) articulates the need for education to be grounded on the cultural basis of the people which recognizes the indigenous knowledge and learning systems.

Scholars all over the world consciously or unconsciously transmit the views, values, beliefs, attitudes, and feelings of their own culture or the society being studied into universal principles assuming that cultures across nations are homogeneous (Phinney & Landin 1998). Although diversity among and within ethnic groups have been identified, due to lack of culture-specific theories in the developing countries and indigenous communities, *Eurocentric*/Euro-American theories are overemphasized in education and classrooms. Local culture which is reflected in language, social norms, customs, rituals and celebrations, morals, beliefs and conventions should be given due consideration, incorporated into theories and classroom lessons to enhance knowledge and understanding for sustainable development (Janetius, Mulat & Mini, 2007).

The projections of Euro-American ideas and their values have been represented as the source of knowledge and guardian of knowledge and their truth-claims are the centre of modern culture. Mohanty (1997) identifies that the major aim of *Eurocentrism* is the projection of European and American interests, concerns, predilections, neuroses, prejudices, social institutions and social categories as the sine qua non of what is right, what is acceptable, what is progressive, what is modern, what is utopian etc. This reckless propaganda of Euro-American interests dispatches an imaginary aura. This aura has been accepted as tangible reality unquestionably for decades by scholars and educationalists of many developing countries and indigenous cultural communities. It is due to the fact that there are no well-defined patterns of scientific knowledge, precise theories of human and social phenomenon, clear concept of political and economical policy, and comprehensive traditional local systems of education. Today, due to developments in the field of technology and the awakened awareness for cultural competency around the globe we need to culture-specific, relativistic approach and application to replace absolute, universal theories.

The conflict between universal theories and their culture-specific application is not new. In the field of psychology, sociology and anthropology the universal vs. culture-specific conflict in application is identified by many scholars (Cooper & Denner, 1998). Internationally, many scholars have raised questions about the cultural assumptions that underlie mainstream and cross-cultural studies and approaches (namely, absolutism and universalism) and have argued for indigenizing theories in human sciences (Sinha, 1997). Although cultural relativism and cross-cultural comparisons are becoming popular ways of studying culture all over the world, resistance for culture-specific studies still resides in the mind of many scholars and educationalists. Resistance to culture-specific study can arise from many factors. It could be science based on reductionism and methodological difficulties, lack of cultural contact or a kind of myopic perspective that neglects focus on cultural uniqueness, dominant political and economical power of the developed countries and, modern day intellectual colonization (Su, 2006). If resistances are overcome, it will lead to indigenization of knowledge, that is, knowing, doing things fit naturally to the environment.

Negligible attempts have been taken in the last few decades to establish African culture as new paradigm of knowledge and education as against the *Eurocentrism*. The attempts failed to gain significant progress due to the Eurocentric educational background of the scholars themselves and their predisposition to see culture in terms of their colonizer's schema, both in research and education. However, a highly esteemed and significant initiative taken by Molefe Asante (1987) for *Afrocentrism* is note worthy. Asante explains *Afrocentricity* in the following way:

> "... we have lost our own cultural footing and become other than our cultural and political origins, dislocated

and disoriented. We are essentially insane, that is, living an absurdity from which we will never be able to free our minds until we return to the source. Afrocentricity as a theory of change intends to re-locate the African person as subject. . . . Afrocentricity becomes the key to the proper education of children and the essence of an African cultural revival and, indeed, survival" (Asante, 1995, p. 1).

Asante's call for *Afrocentrism* to re-locate Africa historically, economically, socially, politically, and philosophically, sounds like a lonely trumpet in the wilderness. Also his initiative has been looked-down by many Euro-American scholars as a political, racist agenda (Palermo, 1997; Lefkowitz, 1996; Walker, 2000). Yet, many scholars who take a moderate view of *Afrocentrism* does not degrade Euro-American concepts and knowledge base, rather raise questions about the undue dominance it takes at the cost of ignoring and disregarding various other knowledge bases (Mkabela, 2005; Alkebulan, 2007). Mkabela (2005) for example, reiterates the need for *Afrocentric* perspective that will provide new insights for understanding African indigenous culture in a multicultural context and, it is a necessary part of complete scholarship without which African scenario is incomplete, less accurate, and less objective.

Besides Asante, many African as well as likeminded scholars explore the possibility of African indigenous knowledge to incorporate into education. Tedla (1995) recommends Sankofan education as an African-centered education because the Euro-American view does not give importance to the traditional African way of life. Semali (1999) campaigns for *Afrocentric* dialectic for African schools, based on indigenous literacy, local culture, language, local innovations and techniques. Mpofu (2002) who studied Zimbabwe people concludes that the concept of intelligence in psychology identified by of Euro-American theories does not fit into African socio-cultural context and requires incorporation of local theories into education. James Banks (1997), a leader in the field of multicultural education, suggests the need for integration of cultural content into curriculum. Papoutsaki (2006) recommends locally informed research culture to create curricula that are based on local knowledge systems and encouraging young people to be more involved in their communities as active participants in the research process.

Imitating or stereotyping western methods becomes a barrier to identifying local values and customs and therefore alternative local human development theories are recommended for Africa in general and Sudan in particular by Hawi (2005). Researches in Ethiopia and other parts of Africa show that the language of instruction plays a vital role in the learning process as well as in the students' performance and native languages have an added advantage (Mekonnen, 2006; Komareck, 2000; Prah, 2003). All these and similar calls make out two things: firstly, a deeper understanding of one's own culture which Freire's (1972) identifies as a process of consciousness raising for increased cultural sensitivity; secondly, a clear understanding of other cultures to look for similarities and differentiate factors.

The uniqueness of Ethiopian socio-cultural context creates

challenges to teachers and scholars due to the questionable accuracy and applicability of *Eurocentric* theories that are being taught in various disciplines in the institutes of higher education in Ethiopia.

- How far cross-cultural theories have soundness for universal application?
- How far the Western theories unassailable for Ethiopian cultural context?

These are some of the exigent questions often raised by scholarly teachers, educationalists as well as critical students. These and other similar questions call for revisiting theoretical bases of knowledge. The questions also highlight the need for indigenous, culture-specific theories, specific mode and frame of knowledge for consequential education.

Although the need for indigenizing education in Africa is becoming a leading issue in the educational circles, there are not many notable initiatives taken in Ethiopia to establish indigenous theories, knowledge base that could be incorporated into curriculum and education. If this is done, it would offer a wonderful basis for cultural responsiveness, socially responsive knowledge as well as culturally responsive learning for consequential education in Ethiopia. In this view, the authors define consequential education in Ethiopia as a process of learning in which the teacher encourages critical examination of multiple sources of knowledge and theories in diverse learning styles with the intention that the acquired knowledge is centered, located, oriented, and grounded on the learner's culture, which could be applied, translated appropriately by the learner and thus well equipped to be productive locally and globally. Common myths regarding *Afro/Ethiocentrism* vs. *Eurocentrism*:

- **Myth 1**: Euro-American way of thinking is the civilized way of thinking. Encouraging local concepts and ideologies will lead the society to backwardness
- **Myth 2**: Euro-American way of doing research is the most accurate, scientific way of doing research. Identifying local modes of data collection are unscientific and unreliable
- **Myth 3:** Euro-American system of education is the best way of education as it is globally spread and universally accepted. When a best system available, why go for indigenous *Afrocentric* models
- **Myth 4**: If contextual culture-specific theories need to standout in the international podium, must follow some universal norms

The myths identified clearly reflect the fact that formal educational set-up and systems originated and spread all over the world from the *Eurocentric* paradigm. This frame of education and the societal conditions and cultural praxis they reflect are universally dominant. However, when applied to other cultures and systems of education, like in Africa, Asia, Latin-America, Oceania or other geographical territories leads to confusion and disparity between what is being taught and what is being lived and practiced in real-life situations. Many Euro-American scholars as well as non-European scholars who claim universal application of their theories and concepts spuriously label many diverse cultural concepts and ideologies which basically differ from their theories and concepts as exceptions and, or limitations. When the uniqueness of different indigenous, culturally different knowledge domains across the globe are ignored, labeled as limitations or minority concepts, many cultural knowledge bases are thrust to the fringe of disappearance, oblivion and annihilation. The irony of this supremacy scenario is that Europe and America constitutes only 17% of world population (figure 2) whose knowledge base dominates the whole world.

Another base for the identified myths comes from the orientation towards studying culture. Orientation towards culture has three distinct perspectives: absolutism, universalism and relativism (Su, 2006). Most Euro-American theories in mainstream sciences claim absolutistic stance. The setback of this approach is that, absolute claims are made without having considered the knowledge bases of diverse cultural, ethnic populations. Many Euro-American theories and concepts fall in this category. The contemporary popular universalistic approach is a critical and comparative study of culture. Even this universalistic orientation, which identifies the cultural variability, studies variations cross-culturally for identifying universal principles. Cultural relativism, however, refines, expands the theories relevant to the predictions, descriptions, and explanations to dissimilar cultures. Relativism promotes various cultural groups' right to follow their own unique paths of development and knowledge bases, unique activities, values and norms. Cultural relativism emphasizes the need for culture-specific approach in which diverse cultures, indigenous groups and knowledge base are accepted and integrated into theories and education. Therefore relativism could be the ideal approach for multicultural studies and indigenizing knowledge base and education, as it accepts and affirms differences in race, ethnicity, religion, language, economics, sexual orientation, gender, and other differences by opposing universalism and ultimately denying absolutism.

Conceptual Model of Indigenization

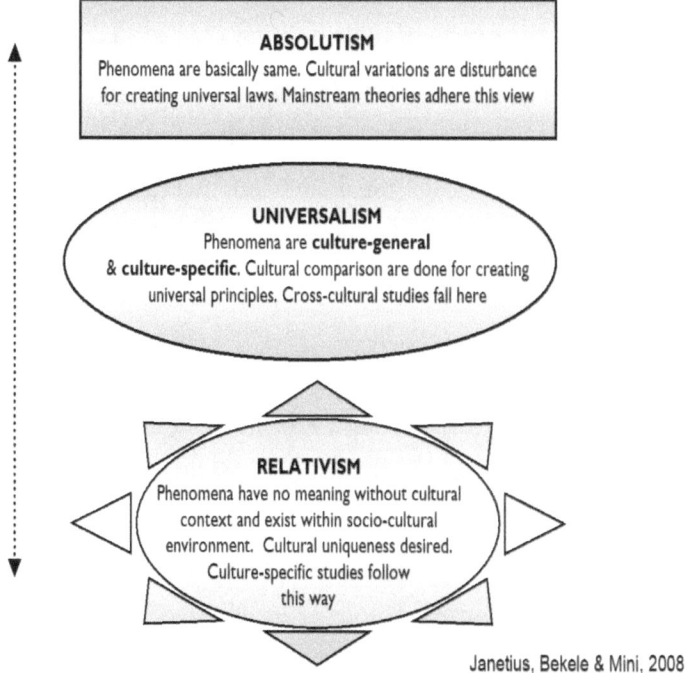

Janetius, Bekele & Mini, 2008

Change is an inevitable reality of life which permeates every sphere of human existence; nothing remains unchanged. As modern scientific developments and lifestyles of alien societies reach indigenous, cultural communities, centuries-old culture, traditional values and customs are fused with the outside culture and new trends emerge. Interaction with another culture or society necessitates changes within one's own culture through adaptations and assimilations in accordance with the changing scenario.

Over the millennia, indigenous people and cultural communities all over the world have developed and sustained practical systems of knowledge and behavior. Evidences clearly correlate cultural, religious praxis, worldview, and lifestyles, provide social support and enhanced coping mechanism for peoples (Janetius, 2003). However, due to international political, religious, intellectual colonialism and an intensified offence by Euro-American socio-economic-political forces through education and mass media, the vital knowledge and skill base has been increasingly displaced. Now marginalized, the indigenous treasures face extinction in most regions of the world.

The authors formulate a *six stage pyramid model* to situate the current indigenization and cultural integration process in Ethiopian education. In the pyramid model, indigenization and cultural integration process moves from top to bottom from *Eurocentrism* towards *Afro/Ethiocentrism* (Ethiopian centered). The six stages are:

  i) initiation
  ii) assimilation
  iii) replication
  iv) realization
  v) indigenization
  vi) integration.

Indigenizing is a process with activities and stages that progress in a very slow rhythm, not limited to indigenous concepts and practices, rather a positive movement towards integration that extends to encompass modern theories, knowledge and methodologies that are used all over the world. The model also implies that if no conscious steps are taken, there are chances that the process may be stunted at any one stage. The narrow top of the pyramid model indicates shallow cultural integration and least indigenization and the broader base implies considerable indigenization and cultural integration.

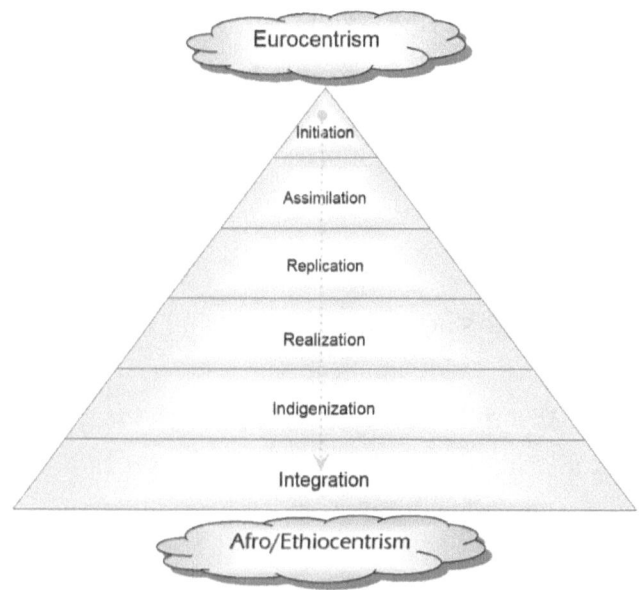

In the ***initiation stage*** the intellectual elite see the greatness of the Euro-American educational system and do their studies. This stage takes place generally when people study in colleges, universities or go abroad for higher studies.

In the ***assimilation stage,*** scholars recognize the relevance of such education for the other people. What they have acquired, they try to introduce in their educational systems in a minimal way.

The **replication stage** is characterized by strong attempts to imitate and reproduce Euro-American knowledge, research, concepts and technologies, in every sphere of education and keep them as standard measures of all intellectual application and thus try to stand out in par with the Euro-American system. This is the most dangerous and damaging period in the pyramid process.

There is very high appreciation for Eurocentric concepts that make the scholars forget the uniqueness and richness of their culture. At this stage the scholars even question the need for culture-specific approaches and disapprove those who try and work for incorporation of indigenous cultural knowledge.

Realization stage starts when the elite and scholars identify the limitations and application deficiencies of Euro-American theories and realize the need for indigenous theories and knowledge base. This is the starting point of indigenization and cultural incorporation.

Indigenization stage is achieved when appreciation for local culture, tradition and knowledge base reaches a high plateau. This is also a period of crisis, in which the meaninglessness and inappropriateness of the *Eurocentric* standards are highly awakened and scholars feel a sense of urgency to create a new local knowledge base, concepts and unique local educational technologies appropriate and meaningful to the land and culture.

Meanwhile, the scholars also feel the anxiety and pain of leaving behind a conventional way in order to create a new world of cultural appropriateness. Once this crisis period is over, a settling period starts in which an ultimate *integration* is achieved. Here, concepts from local knowledge base are given priority and Euro-American and other cultural components are combined and taught in a multicultural way.

If an individual scholar or group of scholars or an institution believes that he/she/they have reached the fourth stage of the above pyramid, the following model of indigenization can be utilized for consequential education.

The model has four parts or stages:

    i) identifying cultural constructs

    ii) extensive qualitative, descriptive research

    iii) ground the research findings

    iv) incorporate theories and knowledge

The first stage is identifying cultural constructs for creating knowledge base. This can be done in the following way: identify Euro-American theories that do not fit into the Ethiopian cultural context and from there, get some clues to identify cultural constructs that needs further exploration.

In the second stage, extensive qualitative, descriptive research is encouraged on the identified constructs of the first stage and other related phenomena. The research is not focused on to show the percentage and degree of the phenomena being studied but to explain the phenomena in an *emic* way which will pave way for creation of theories and local knowledge base. In the third stage, ground the research findings to define local knowledge base, local philosophy, theories etc... which can replace the out-of-context Euro-American theories.

In the final stage, incorporate the theories and knowledge into teaching and curriculum in order to make the education consequential. Also, the cultural constructs in the first stage as well as the researches could be indirectly incorporated into curriculum and teaching for consequential education. It is a slow but steady process that leads the educational system, once completely dependent on another cultural basis and model, to grow to maturity and become independent and flourish.

Education is a multi-dimensional tool and the development of educational systems is the outcome of long processes. Culture plays a crucial role in making education meaningful, purposeful and consequential. Without integrating cultural components, local knowledge base into education, it becomes a ritual and fruitless.

In order to make education consequential the limitations of Euro-American theories that are taught in our institutions of higher education, which needs indigenization. Also, many local cultural constructs that need extensive research so that local knowledge base could be established and local theories formulated. The need for qualitative research in many human and social sciences, other related fields to create local theories that explain human phenomena in Ethiopia should be given high priority so that education can be indigenized. This measured time-consuming steady process needs serious consideration now. If not the education system will be under intellectual colonization of Euro-American systems, without local identity and individuality.

Recommendations: A local centre for indigenous research should be established and dedicated to fulltime descriptive studies of cultural concepts and cultural constructs so that *Ethiocentric* theories can be formed and incorporated into education. Thus local indigenous data and knowledge base would be available in different levels of education. It appears that, for many teachers to have a shift to *Afro/Ethiocentrism* is difficult because they were grown up in Eurocentric education system. Therefore, adequate pedagogical training in the form of refresher courses could be organized periodically.

It is also good for other researchers in this field to use the findings of this research as a stepping stone to indigenize knowledge on a broader scale by including more variables. The proposed conceptual model could be used to indigenize knowledge base so that, the conceptual model could be validated further and its applicability could be explored elaborately.

The following suggestions can be given serious considerations:

1. A local center for indigenous research should be established and dedicated to fulltime descriptive studies of cultural concepts and cultural constructs so that *Ethiocentric* theories can be formed and incorporated into education. Thus local indigenous data and

knowledge base would be available in different levels of education. To this end (in order to facilitate indigenized consequential education), the Ministry of Education should take strong initiatives

2. It appears that, for many teachers to have a shift to *Afro/Ethiocentrism* is difficult because they were grown up in *Eurocentric* education system. Therefore, adequate pedagogical training in the form of refresher courses could be organized periodically.

3. It is also good for other researchers in this field to use the findings of this research as a stepping stone to indigenize knowledge on a broader scale by including more variables. The proposed conceptual model could be used to indigenize knowledge base so that, the conceptual model could be validated further and its applicability could be explored elaborately.

CHAPTER TWELVE

Transpersonal Psychotherapy

The word transpersonal comes from two words - *trans* (beyond or through) and *persona* (mask or façade). Transpersonal approach in psychology used to refer to any human experience related to religion, spirituality, meditation and mysticism (Daniels, 1998). However, today it covers a wider variety of phenomena, not necessarily religious or spiritual. Transpersonal psychology studies phenomena like mystical states of consciousness, meditative practices, shamanic states, rituals etc in a psychological context (Silva, 2001). It is also a process of harmonious blending of religion and spiritual experiences in psychology. From the many definitions and views of transpersonal psychology, Lajoie & Shapiro (1992) identify the following five elements as the basic characteristics of transpersonal psychology. They are:(a) an interest in states of consciousness, (b) concern with humanity's highest or ultimate potential, (c) human experience that goes beyond ego or personal self, (d) the idea of transcendence, and (e) a spiritual dimension in human life.

The study of transpersonal psychology starts with William James and his study of mystical experiences. James pointed out that mystical experiences are the basis or starting point for all the world's religions (James, 1936). On the contrary, Freud considered religion as infantile neurosis and dismissed mystical experiences as fantasies and regressions to a womb-like state (Freud, 1928); the behaviorists ruled out the possibility of scientific study of any of these experiences to be empirical in their approach. However, Carl Jung showed special interest in mystical and transpersonal issues. In contrast to Freud who labeled religion as an illusion and religious experiences as infantile neurosis, Jung considered spiritual experiences as a sign of mental health and relief from neurosis (Jung, 1989).

Jung also postulates that every human person is endowed with potentials for transpersonal and mystical experiences. His theory on personality which talks about collective unconscious, archetypes, such as the self, shadow, hero, and the divine child that are related to dreams, rituals, and other symbols in life are clear signs of the mystical nature of human beings (Jung, 1958). Abraham Maslow, the founder of humanistic psychology, is considered one of the pioneers of transpersonal psychology. The great importance Maslow gave to self-actualization, peak experiences and plateau experiences as the highest attainable motivations and goals of humans, see him as the great explorer of the transpersonal in human beings (Walsh & Vaughan, 1993). Maslow sees transpersonal psychology as the logical leap beyond humanistic Psychology and nicknamed it *Fourth-force Psychology* in relation to psychoanalysis, behaviorism, and humanistic psychology, and considered it a stage higher than humanistic psychology (Hendricks & Weinhold, 1982). In the theories of Carl Rogers, Fritz Perls and Viktor Frankle too, transpersonal ideas are seen although not identified purely as such.

Besides psychologists, many scientists and great scholars have given great importance to transpersonal view of human behavior and existence:- Aldous Huxley and Stan Grof who conducted investigations into altered consciousness using Mescaline, LSD and other Psychedelics; Teilhard de Chardin, who integrated biology with Christian theology to develop a model of cosmic consciousness; Sri Aurobindo, the Indian Mystic who talked about the evolution of consciousness based on Indian philosophies; Roberto Assagioli, the founder of *psychosynthesis* - are just a few of the many we could mention.

Today, Ken Wilber, who integrates the philosophies and psychologies of East and West, ancient and modern, in developing his *Spectrum Theory of Consciousness* is one of the leading theorists in transpersonal. According to Wilber (1983): "The material body is exercised in labor with the physical-natural environment; the *pranic* (emotional) body is exercised in breath, sex, and feeling with other *pranic* bodies; the mind is exercised in linguistic communication with other minds; the soul, in psychic and subtle relationships; the spirit, in absolute relation to and as Godhead (or God-communion and God-identity). That is, each level of the compound human individual is exercised in a complex system of ideally unobstructed relationships with the corresponding levels of structural organization in the world process at large" (pp. 35-36). The focus of Wilber's transpersonal approach is to have a holistic approach to life and existence. Holism, according to him is the integration of body, mind and spirit; when it is applied in transpersonal therapy, it considers healing from the point of view of the personal integration of three aspects of a person, physical, mental and spiritual (Daniels, 1997).

A transpersonal approach sees human beings as intuitive, mystical, psychic and spiritual (Hendricks & Weinhold, 1982). Psychology considers development and the formation of a stable, integrated, and individuated ego as the goal of human development and mental health whereas transpersonal psychology exceeds such description of psychological theories and explores stages of personality development that extend beyond the individual ego into transpersonal realms (Wilber, 2000). *However, it is important to distinguish bizarre phenomenon from transpersonal experience or phenomenon.* Daniels (1998) argues that any event, experience, or phenomenon that has a transformational meaning or effect on a person can be considered subject matter for transpersonal psychology. Therefore, wide ranges of paranormal experiences are included in the subject matter of transpersonal psychology.

It is not necessary to be a follower of any religion to use transpersonal approach in counseling and psychotherapy. In the first place, as counselors and therapists, be aware that people have their own unique view of the cosmos, worldview, health concepts and healing practices originating from their specific culture, traditional wisdom; identify them and focus therapy modality accordingly (Janetius, 2003). Second, respect and accept the personal experiences of the clients. Finally identify the client's specific concepts and views regarding healing and try to combine therapy and healing; generally prayer, customary rituals and reconciliation (with self & others) are the main spiritual factors seen among many people all over the world that could be easily adoptable for a transpersonal psychotherapy.

Some specific techniques: If the client relies on factors outside his or her ordinary ego to facilitate healing, ask the client to close the eyes and visualize them for healing. If the client is religious, some form of reconciliation with God, forgiveness of God could be suggested. Prayer and meditation could be encouraged because many charismatic prayer experiences of Christians are similar to catharsis and, meditation brings out the same effects of imagery and relaxation techniques. A word of promise 'I will pray for you...' will bring enormous amount of positive feelings and confidence that can extra-boost the healing process. If the client has no religious beliefs, focus on some values and spirituality of the client (doing justice, possessing rationality and free will to decide etc...). Help the client re-establish a conscious relationship with self and others by different modalities applicable and acceptable to the individual. Do not focus on the issue (presenting problem or symptoms), rather on the belief system of the client (presenting problem vs. real problem), identify the problems from the point of client's worldview. Facilitate and help the client to build new patterns of thought, feeling and behavior (like the one commonly used by cognitive therapists) by way of meditation, visualization and autosuggestion, based on the belief system either religious or spiritual. Therapeutic touch (in which the therapist touches the client) which is one of the earliest and widely seen healing practices all over the world and traditions, can create wide range of positive impacts in the client

The transpersonal approach recognizes the importance of integrative aspects in which many disciplines like philosophy, psychiatry, counseling and psychotherapy, sociology, politics, education, anthropology, history, literary studies, religious studies, biology and physics merge together. It embraces an oriental worldview that incorporates elements of personal mysticism, native philosophy, worldview and cosmology. Thus it is very much in tune with meditation, yoga, shamanic and traditional healings, therapeutic touch, raiki, acupuncture, and other supernatural, mystical and psychic experiences. It could be very well integrated into mainstream psychotherapy and counseling, provided the counselor or therapist is very intuitive, creative and skilled.

CHAPTER THIRTEEN

Culture-Specific Therapy

Ethiopia is a country of deep rooted traditions and religious practices dating back to the history of King Solomon in the Bible. Ethiopian society is also known for many traditional healing practices often mixed with Christian, Muslim and other traditional religious and shamanic rituals. Western models of Counseling and psychotherapy are new to the people. Traditional healing methods are widely used to treat physical as well as psychological illness in Ethiopia. Mental Health is one of the most disadvantaged health programs in Ethiopia, both in terms of facilities and trained manpower. In the traditional Ethiopian worldview, illness of any kind is often associated with forces of witchcraft, evil eye and other believed negative forces and the healing process is often done by priests and other religiomagical healers of one or other religion and category. The Western form of counseling or psychotherapy is not popular in the country, although rapid expansion is seen in the recent years in school counseling and VCT services for HIV in cities and urban centers. However, it has not penetrated into the rural areas.

Due to the strong religious background, people always look for religiomagical solutions to their problems. Therefore preparing an indigenous counseling model by incorporating the existing traditional modalities would be a real challenge to the psychologists and clinicians in Ethiopia. The unique traditional

Ethiopian worldview and the human developmental psychological functions of the people demand for a cultural-sensitive counseling and psychotherapeutic approaches which are tailor-made for the people in Ethiopia. Counselling psychology is limited to school, colleges and VCT centers today need to expand to all mental health issues. Awareness about mental health issues together with indigenous counseling models will bring the country to a better future.

Ethiopia is home to more than 80 ethnic groups. The Oromo (34.49%) in the Southern part and Amhara (26.89%) in the central highlands are the two most populous groups and other groups counting less than 10% total population and some are as few as 10,000 members (ECSA, 2007). The main languages used in the country are Amharic, Oromiffa, and Tigrinya. Amharic, the official language of the government, has its origin in the Semitic roots and Oromiffa is Cushitic. The medium of instruction in primary schools across the country was Amharic which has been replaced by local languages in many places as the result of socio-political movements for the rights of children to learn in their vernaculars. English is taught in all secondary schools and it is the medium of instruction in the higher learning institutions.

Ethiopia has a long history of Hebrew religious background. The two religious groups that dominate the country's belief system are Christianity and Islam. The predominant Orthodox Christianity in Ethiopia has its roots in the King Solomon dynasty of the Old Testament. The Muslim influence in the country goes back to the time of earliest disciples of the prophet Mohammed, who during persecution in Arabia, found refuge in Abyssinia. Also, the first mosque in Africa was built in the Tigre province, in the northern Ethiopia. The adherents of animist religions inhabit mainly in the southernmost regions and also remote villages all over the country. A small Jewish community, although most of them have migrated to Israel, still holds some remnants in the highlands of Gondar town in the Northern Ethiopia.

Indigenous and traditional healing methods: Magic, religion, health and well-being are all mixed up in the primitive societies. It is very difficult to differentiate animist, shamanic healing from religious, magical and herbal healings. In the traditional cultures, the mixture of herbal concoction together with religious rituals, rites and magic like formulas were part of every healing practice. Ethiopian society is not an exception to these traditional health concepts. Traditional healing practices in Ethiopia are often mingled with Christian, Muslim and other primitive animist, shamanic rituals.

Health and wellbeing in Ethiopia are understood as a state of equilibrium among physiological, religious, cosmological, ecological, and social factors surrounding the lives of people. This holistic outlook of wellbeing arises from the worldview of the people that good health is a gift of God and evil forces can deter it. Similar popular beliefs regarding health and sickness are: the supernatural forces can enter a person's body to disturb the health; the shadows cast by an evil eye could be the source of sickness; environmental hazards, poor hygiene and climatic conditions for example heat, rain or cold wind can cause illness.

Consequently, this worldview does not differentiate psychological or mental illness and related wellbeing as a separate entity from that of physiological. Owing to this traditional life-world, people indiscriminately go to priests or religiomagical healers, sorcerers and other kinds of traditional healers for each and every sickness physical, psychological or emotional. Obviously, psychiatric and mental health services are very scarce in the country. Even where it is available or accessible, people do not feel free to utilize the services (Desalew & Yigzaw, 2007). People resort to modern mental health medical services only after they have tried and failed one or other traditional healing covertly or overtly.

Another factor that contributes to the popularity of traditional religiomagical healings would be the fact that modern medicines (Western medicines) and health care facilities are throttled to the cities and towns. These facilities are available meagerly in towns and a vast majority of the population has no access to this. The national average physician to population ratio is 1:510425 where as the Orthodox Christian priest ratio is 1: 1006 and it is no wonder that the local population seeks traditional medicine from orthodox priests more than doctors (Mini, 2008). These traditional religious healings are available in every village or nearby, easily accessible - socially, economically and geographically.

Today in Ethiopia up to 80% of the population uses traditional healing practices in one or the other way (ECSA, 2001). Many of these traditional healing practices are interwoven with Ethiopian Orthodox Christianity or other religious practices. Scholars are of different opinion in classifying traditional healing practices as well as naming traditional healers in Ethiopia (Kebede, et al., 2006). However, the traditional healing practices could be classified broadly into two major categories:

1) Orthodox Christian healings

2) Shamanic traditional healings

The Orthodox Christian traditional healings could be further categorized into three:

a) medicine men/women and herbalists

b) religiomagical healers, primarily the Orthodox priests

c) *debteras* (defrocked orthodox Christian priests)

The second category which is more of shamanic in nature popularly practiced by animists, Muslims as well as secretly by Christians. They are:

i) *tenquay* (witch doctors)

ii) weqaby and *kalicha*

iii) *zar* healings by specialists called *awaky balazar*

There is no uniformity in the healing practices among this second category of healers except the basic philosophy that sickness is caused by some external forces.

The orthodox Christian healings originate from the belief that health is a gift of God and, evil forces can cause sicknesses. The primary form of well-accepted religiomagical healing for every Orthodox Christian is the Holy Water or *tsebel*. Churches and healing places are crowded with plastic cans and bottles of water, queued to be blessed by the priest and then used for drinking, washing, rubbing and sprinkling as part of healing. Another popular healing method often closely associated with religious healing is ritual baptism, fasting and penance. Priests prescribe these as part of healing or the people themselves voluntarily do this for healings.

Besides priests, it is the *debtera*s and *yekolo tamari* (priestly candidate) who control the religiomagical healings. *Debteras* participate in the liturgy as singers and musicians and, outside the church employ themselves as healers in the form of herbalists, magical healers, astrologers, fortune-tellers etc. Some Ethiopian authors consider these healers as spiritual healers whereas in many standards they are purely religiomagical healers. They do their healing practices in the name of religion and attribute one or another magical element attached to their healing methodology.

A major theological difference in the healing practices of priests and *debteras* is that, for the priests, sin vs. virtue and evil-spirit vs. God is the basic platform for identification of any sickness and as well as healings. Therefore they prescribe prayer (*degmit*), holy water (*tsebel*), baptism (washing of sins), fasting, or penance as a remedy. For the *debteras* it is always evil spirit vs. human beings; almost all the sickness are possession of evil spirits or caused by evil spirits, therefore, prayer (*degmit*) and holy water (*tsebel*) become the integral part of any ritualistic religious ceremony, together with some magical healing practices.

Kitab or amulets are the popular remedial safety weapon prepared and given by the *debteras* to be worn to wade away the evil spirits and evil eye (*buda*). On the other hand the priests encourage the practice of confession, fasting, penance, Church attendance and *kurban* (communion) as a means of healing together with some sort of advice and guidance.

Zar and other shamanic healings originate from the belief that illness is the outcome of malevolent spirits. These possessions are identified collectively as *kureyna*. When people believe the symptoms of sickness as indications of possession of spirit, the customary remedy would be consulting an *awakiy balazar* (shamanic healer) who in turn would propose traditional therapy for possession by shamanic trance. Sometimes the patient need to stay in the house of the *awakiy balazar* for a longer period of time, if the possessed spirit does not communicate its identity. The patients are given chat (stimulant leaves) and directed to follow a regulated courses of diet until the identity of the possessed spirit is revealed. In order to appease the spirit, periodic gifts such as perfumes, clothes, and Jewells are demanded. The therapy administered by the *awakiy balazar* is not curing, but socializing or taming the disturbing spirit by another spirit owned by the healer or called by the healer.

As far as the herbal healing is considered, there are very few herbalists in the country who can clearly identify the right herbals or mastered the knowledge fully the healing herbals. However, today it is a common practice among many traditional healers to call themselves herbalists. This is simply because the government requires a license to practice traditional healing. The government issues licenses only to herbalists who use plants and herbs. This led to the artificial transformation of herbal healers everywhere which in fact none other than religiomagical healers, witch doctors and *zar* healers in disguise. The traditional healers as well as local people believe that the ability to heal is God given and it should be kept in maximum secret. Often, the knowledge is passed orally from generation to generation and also safeguarded by certain group of people as family tradition and prestige. This secrecy becomes a barrier for this healing art to spread further.

The traditional healing practices of priests, *debteras* and other traditional healers have a lot of similarity to Western models of counseling and psychotherapy although not understood or labeled as counseling and psychotherapy in the modern sense. These traditional healings involve active listening, empathy, person-centered approach in understanding the problems of the clients which are important components of Western counseling and psychotherapy. Besides these, a popular practice among Ethiopian Orthodox Christians called soul-father *'yenafsabbat'*, that is accepting a priest as family counselor or spiritual-doctor and mentor, who makes frequent visits to homes and families to carry out guidance services could be ascertained as an equivalent to Western therapist-client relationship and therapeutic process. It is this process that makes the traditional healing more attractive to people over modern medicines and therapy modalities.

Counseling was introduced in Ethiopia in early 1960's, not as a therapy modality but as an educational tool. As a part of educational training and to enhance better understanding of pupil, psychological testing, measurement and evaluation were taught in the College of Education. One of the notable persons offering the course of Counseling Psychology at Addis Ababa

University was Dr. David Cox from the University of Utah, USA.

Psychological counseling in Ethiopia took new dimensions, a way beyond education primarily due to the global awareness on increasing number of HIV cases in Africa. Voluntary Counseling and Testing (VCT) centers discuss the reasons for testing and prepare the clients to accept the test results either positive or negative. It is generally a single session assistance to clients and not much to do with therapy as such. Secondly, the modernization of higher education by the Federal Government of Ethiopia together with the United Nations Development Program paved the way for Ethiopian scholars to go abroad for higher studies. Their return started a small new beginning in the field of counseling and psychotherapy by opening counseling services in the universities and colleges. Nonetheless, counseling services in the colleges have not brought the desired outcome. In a study conducted on the counseling services offered in one of the Ethiopian Universities, studying 873 students i.e. roughly 10% of the population, it was identified that the counseling services were offered by the psychology department teachers as part-time basis and the student counselor ratio was 1: 1746. In spite of the fact that the students were given orientation and informed about the counseling services in the college, only 68% of the surveyed students know about the services in the university. It is also surprising to know that in a student population of more than 8, 000 only 30 students came for counseling assistance in a period of six months. None of the students who got counseling assistance were referred by the teachers rather they came by hearsay (Janetius & Bekele, 2007). This shows the fact that current status of counseling and psychotherapy, although introduced in a small way, has not penetrated into the minds of the students as a therapy modality.

In spite of the fact that 450 to 500 students graduate in psychology per annum, only a very few choose their profession as therapeutic counselors. Those who practice counseling are often seen working in VCT centers or in high schools and colleges offering guidance services without following any specific theory or approaches. There is only one specialized mental health hospital at Addis Ababa where counseling and psychotherapy are practiced purely as a therapy modality.

Counselor education has taken new dimensions in Ethiopia due to the expansion of higher education in unison with the United Nations Development Program. Having just one university two decades ago, Ethiopian higher education sector has leaped today to thirty one universities, out of which more than ten offer psychology at the undergraduate level. Addis Ababa University, the first university in Ethiopia that offered psychology in the department of education is now offering Masters Program in counseling psychology. Steps have been taken to begin PhD program in counseling psychology. Almost all the universities offering undergraduate psychology course have two papers in counseling psychology, one theory and another practicum.

The beginning of counseling psychology as a therapy modal in the curriculum of college education, as well as offering counseling services to the students in a minimal way, has its positive and negative sides. In the positive note, we see counseling slowly spreads beyond the umbrella of education as a mental health therapy model. However, the major negative side would be, the Western theories and approaches are unscrupulously taught as the only way of understanding human behavior and mental illness and, so far no initiatives taken to incorporate and integrate traditional concepts and healing modalities into counseling and psychotherapy. No steps have been taken to identify some culture-specific psychological systems and therapy, which are uniquely Ethiopian, for better reach out. Also, counseling and psychotherapy has not taken professional attire in Ethiopia and therefore there is no licensing and certification system for psychologists, counselors or psychotherapists.

Professional education programs of the colleges and universities have accreditation by the Higher Education Relevance and Quality Agency (HERQA, 2007) which has been regularly monitoring quality under the auspicious guidance of the Ministry of Education. It is conducted by the general scheme of control of quality and licensing in the higher learning institutions in the country. Its mission is to ensure a higher quality and relevant higher education system in Ethiopia (Tesfaye & Kassahun, 2009).

Ethiopian government requires license for traditional healers to practice. Although it was much stricter during the Derg regime that was in power until 1987, today majority of the healers in the rural areas do not adhere to this regulation. In 1991, the Bio-Diversity Institute which is governed by the Ministry of Agriculture has organized an Association of Traditional Healers to identify the healing herbs and preserve them in the country. The members of this association are also entitled to get a working license to practice healing by using herbal medicine. It is very common these days to see in Addis Ababa, the capital city of the country and other major cities, signposts advertising licensed herbal healers. However, many of these healers in fact practice religiomagical healings, sorcery and witchcraft under the cover of licensed herbalists. In the coming years, once counseling is accepted as a full-fledged healing and therapy modality, licensing and accreditation could be expected for counselors.

In spite of the fact that scholars all over the world highlight the need for indigenous psychology and culture-specific approaches, Western models of therapy are currently used in Ethiopia due to lack of available local theories and therapy models. In the Ethiopian institutes of higher education, Western theories and approaches in the field of counseling and psychotherapy are formally taught. The applicability of such theories and approaches in the Ethiopian context is not questioned by the local scholars. Although there is an emerging trend and overall awareness to integrate culture and worldview into education and curriculum, a strong culture-sensitive approach to assessment and diagnosis is not augmented so far. Counselors generally prefer to claim that they use an eclectic approach. From the experience of guiding and training students in counseling psychology, it is understood that among all the Western models of counseling, psychodynamic approach is the least preferred approach whereas behavioral-cognitive approach and humanistic approaches are the most popular among psychology students. Wherever transpersonal approach is taught, the students show liking for that model too.

The indigenous traditional healing practices can contribute a lot for better counseling processes in Ethiopia. Many traditional healers adhere to essential characteristics of a good therapist using wonderful counseling techniques like better communication, listening skills, rapport building, empathy etc., and certain postulates could be drawn from these traditional methods and healers to enhance culture-specific counseling and psychotherapy. A fine integration of religious elements, cultural components, worldview and belief system into local frameworks of mental health and therapeutic interventions, is the need of the time, as against the Western doctrines and therapeutic models.

The traditional healing practices and the related belief system have a lot of treasures that needs further exploration in the field of psychology in general and counseling in particular. The need for integration of such identified elements from traditional healings into culture-specific approach is important for counseling and psychotherapy to emerge as a therapy modality and to have professional attire. The beginning of counseling psychology programs at undergraduate level in many universities in the country and the global awareness and greater emphasis on culture specific therapy models could change the situation in Ethiopia in the course of time.

A culture-sensitive approach in psychology is very important in this era of globalization, when Western knowledge base is often projected as the only choice for many people around the world regardless of different unique heritage and culture. Lack of culture-specific therapeutic approaches and commonly taught

Western model of therapy could be a major challenge for the development of counseling and psychotherapy in Ethiopia. Clinicians apply some form of eclectic approach without incorporating the unique traditions and culture of the society. As the Ethiopian psyche is basically religiously mooted, some forms of transpersonal therapy together with some indigenous practices could be an ideal choice in the Ethiopian context as it values and integrates the personal and transpersonal, the psychological and spiritual aspects.

Misperceptions about the cause and treatment of psychological problems and mental illness, help seeking behavior, fear of stigma, and lack of awareness about counseling and psychotherapy services could be another challenge and shows the weaker side of working professionals in the field of counseling. The Ethiopian psychological association and similar bodies can work to raise awareness among the public by regular awareness programs in the grassroots. Research activities need to be focused on creating an indigenous psychology and counseling in the country that will give counseling psychology a bright future.

The prisoner's story- a case study: This is a case of a young prisoner who was convicted 16 years imprisonment at the age of 19. The counselor was a practicum student in Counseling Psychology under the direct supervision of a qualified counselor.

The Client is a male orthodox Christian born in a poor rural family. His parents are farmers. He has two younger sisters and two older ones. His first elder sister is married and has children. His second elder sister left his house few years ago and the client has no knowledge about her whereabouts. His two younger sisters are living with his parents in their native village. From his childhood the client was taking care of family cattle, grazing them in the fields. Since his family is poor he did not get any chance to go to school. He also helped his father in the farming. Few years ago, his father asked him to take care of himself and to go for work outside. He started to work for other persons in the village as a daily worker. Also, he was taking care of their family cattle whenever time permits. He used to get roughly 100 birr (10-15$) every month from his hard labor which he used to share with the family.

The origin of client's problem goes back to couple years when he was attracted by a young girl who was also looking after cows in the fields. As the client explains, "she was so nice, I really liked her and she also loved me". His friends regularly encouraged him as well as forced him in a friendly way to have sex with his girl friend. Even they started to gossip among themselves that he already had sex with her.

One day, while drinking local alcohol with his friends, they encouraged him to have sex with her and client thought that he would give a try. The client went to the field, met her and explained to her about his love and desire. According to his own words, "she also expressed her love for me and I gave her 5 Birr (money equaling less than a dollar) as a gift. She allowed me to touch her, caress her and showed her willingness to have sex". Since she was a virgin, when he had sex she started to bleed. Seeing the blood the girl cried and rushed to her home immediately. The client did not bother much about this incident because he was drunk at the time. Latter he was reprimanded by the girl's family and they filed a complaint in the nearby police station. Finally he was arrested by the police for rape. The case was referred to the court and he was given 16 years of imprisonment for raping a minor girl (since the girl was only 14 years old at the time he had sex). Problems did not stop here for the client. While he was under police custody, his mother died and the police officer did not allow him to visit his home to see his deceased mother and to say good bye to her. The client is also angry towards his father for the reason that he did not negotiate with the girl's family or initiate any compromise before the case was filed in the court. Added to that, his father never visited him in the prison after his arrest and imprisonment.

The following problems were narrated by the client when the counselor met him first: Sleeplessness, hatred for himself and other prisoners, guilt feeling, exaggerated grief over the loss of his mother as well as his absence in the funeral ceremony, angry over the law and prison regulations, loneliness due to lack of interpersonal relationship with the prison inmates, feeling of emptiness, and high suicidal tendency. Although he was in the prison for 11 months, at the time of Counselor's first visit, the client has not accepted the punishment mentally arguing that he has not committed rape rather it was an act of mutual consent. He also thinks strongly that his imprisonment is the outcome of treachery of the girl and her parents, also his parent's inability to negotiate.

The approach taken by the counselor was existential-humanistic approach in helping the client to realize his current situation. Specifically, logotherapy was used to help the client. The main focus of counseling was to help the client to realize his present condition, to have a right orientation and ability to look beyond his immediate problems and daily events. Specific techniques used were: De-reflection and orientation towards meaning.

The client responded positively to the counseling intervention. Since the client had problems in accepting the punishment, de-reflection was useful to substitute something positive in to his life and the technique worked quickly. The client's disorganized attitudes, negative feelings and thoughts towards his future life, hopeless and worthless feelings, suicidal tendency were helped by re-orienting his life towards meaning. Although the client slowly recovered in the first few sessions of counseling, there was no much progress in the latter sessions.

At this period, the counselor was requested by the practicum guide to integrate some Ethiopian traditional practices into counseling sessions. Accordingly, the client was asked whether he would be interested to talk to a priest. The client showed lot of enthusiasm to talk to a priest. Two sessions were arranged with the help of an Orthodox priest from a nearby Church. The client confessed to the priest all the crimes he committed in his life and asked the priest for some penance. After these two sessions and a rapid change was seen in the client. He started to for education classes in the prison for those prisoners who never went to school, he joined traditional cloths weaving and embroidery works class and above all accepted the punishment and started to have hope that there is life after 16 years of imprisonment.

In this case, the client's specific concepts and views regarding healing, especially his religious beliefs were combined with counseling. That is, together with counseling, the client was initiated to prayer, customary rituals and some forms of reconciliation (with self & others) which are part of Ethiopian Orthodox Christian daily living. This kind of simple combination is possible in transpersonal therapy which works well with clients of similar belief.

Postscript

When I was presenting a paper in a conference in India, I compared a research data from Ethiopia with an Indian data and the chair person bluntly commented that how come a data from an underdeveloped country like Ethiopia is comparable with the far more developed India. Of course, no two countries can be compared. No two cultures can be compromised. I was in fact comparing just to show the cultural difference. But the tone in which the scholar commented shocked me. From my experience, I am sure that some of the universities in Ethiopia are much better in infrastructure and facilities and, many of the Ethiopian higher education students are keen on acquiring knowledge than their counterparts in India.

Ethiopia is equally rich in culture and with an equal vigor the Ethiopian government is working to uplift the educational system. There are wonderful teachers who are much better than Indian counterparts in their quest for knowledge. Majority of the scholars in Ethiopia acquire their higher education in America, India and in the European countries and they are much higher in their sphere of understanding and approach to education than many Indian counterparts. The facilities in the Ethiopian universities, the collection of books in the libraries and other infrastructures are way ahead of many of the colleges and private deemed universities in India. The shocking recent incident in India where the

Government of India derecognize 44 universities in the country, is a blatant example of this phenomenon.

My stay in Ethiopia was one of the most amazing experiences in my life. It enabled my development as a culture-specific psychologist, an educationalist, and above all a mature person. I owe a lot to Ethiopia for my growth as a multicultural psychologist too. It opened my eyes to new vistas in understanding different cultures, worldview and people. I visited a lot of places, meet wonderful people, had some remarkable experiences. I did some inspiring researches that paved the way for my growth as a professional psychologist. This book is the outcome of my magnificent experience in Ethiopia. Doing research as a team and presenting them in research forums with my Ethiopian as well as Indian colleagues were memorable events, which I will cherish till my death.

Some of my unforgettable experiences include, preparing Abyssinian coffee, my first ritual in the morning in the backdrop of singing birds; walking up the hill to my campus, a daily forced exercise that kept body weight under control; going for a evening walk meeting innocent simple children in the country side who shout 'YOU ...' and for which I shout back *ante*; noise pollution by the Orthodox Church and the priest's abrasive singing in the wee hours.

As the readers might have understood from the first chapter, my visit to the holy city of Aksum and the ruined palace of Queen of Sheba was a fantastic experience; visit to Lalibella and the incredible ancient Churches never go out of my mind; the ruined castles in Gondar, the highlands of northern Ethiopia, barren landscapes here and there, beautiful lakes, hot springs in the rift-valley, green virgin forestland in the Southern Nations remain with me forever. I experienced Scott Peck's *'Road Less Traveled'* in this African cradle of civilization.

No field is better equipped to meet the challenges of cultural diversity than psychology. The influence of culture in human behavior and thinking is tremendous. Culture influences the language we speak, our perceptions of the world, our thought process, behaviors and attitudes, education, governance, religion and our health. Across all the topics covered in this book the authors elucidated how culture plays a vital role in the ancient as well as modern life of Ethiopians. The studies presented in this simple book through culture-specific contextual studies explain the influence of culture. The absolutism that does not accommodate individual cultural significance creates vacuum in the local knowledge base. On the other hand cross-cultural studies generate a way of understanding truth and principles within a global perspective. Cross-cultural research not only tests similarities and differences in behaviors, it also evaluates possible limitations of our traditional knowledge. Above all, it is culture-specific research that brings out the uniqueness of people and culture without comparisons.

Much of current psychology as a science is a byproduct of western ways of thinking and understanding of human behavior, without considering cultural diversity. The entire scientific process and its products-the theories and models that summarize our understanding of human behavior-are themselves bound and limited by the cultural contexts in which they were derived and existed. These theories and the procedures used to test them may or may not have relevance to people in other cultures.

This volume, Abyssinia in the New Millennium, culture and higher education, initiated by Dr. Janetius and his colleagues, organized to present a variety of topics and issues in a greater detail and comprehensiveness. The topics discussed would substantially contribute to the field of culture specific psychology and education as the book inspires different scholars of different disciplines to further analyze the influence of culture in human behavior, thinking and indigenous knowledge base development.

Dr. Janetius initiated this reality by his simple example of Freudian Psychosexual theory to showcase the fact that Freudian and similar theories of Psychological importance and related concepts reflect and depict the society in which the theorists lived in a particular time and culture. Therefore, it cannot be universally applied. Applying the psychosexual development theory in the Ethiopian context without due consideration for local culture, customs and praxis creates confusion and conflict in the mind of the learners and the knowledge remains in book level, far from applicable understanding. Human development that takes place in a specific cultural, environmental and social conditions of the people that cannot be concluded and established universally.

As discussed briefly in part two and three of the book, teaching in a college and sitting in a college classroom becomes a challenge.

Due to the fact that the lessons and lectures do not share the life-world of the students, do not focus on the culture of the society in which they are born and brought up. As clearly defined in the book,

'Culture-sensitive classroom is that in which the teacher compares and contrasts knowledge cross-culturally and multi-culturally, integrates materials, concepts, and values of local culture into pedagogy and imparts that knowledge in the unique learning style of the learner. Knowledge should be taught from the cultural base of the learner. Therefore, Local culture which is reflected in language, social norms, customs, rituals and celebrations, morals, beliefs and conventions should be given due consideration, incorporated into theories and classroom lessons to enhance knowledge and understanding for sustainable development.

The book ignites this idea in the minds of all readers in many chapters in higher education and integrating culture. If the minds of the readers catch fire while reading this book, the intention of authors are well-taken. It is clear that cultural changes do occur due to a various factors and all the more when cultural labels no longer describe a majority of the individuals within a culture. For instance, the unique cultural practice '*Warsa*' of Workie people in Ethiopia is slowly vanishing due to the increased awareness caused by education and government propaganda against sexually transmitted diseases. However in rural areas where there is illiteracy and less urban influence, it is still practiced as an accepted custom.

More importantly, we need to mend universals and specifics to help us formulate guiding principles that can be used as resources in developing new culture-specific concepts. As it is indicated in part two of this book, Multiple intelligence Theory formalized and introduced by Howard Gardner continues to open the minds of educators, psychologists and the people to upgrade learning so that the students may be better guided to achieve maximum intellectual potential. Taking into consideration the multiple intelligence theory of Gardner the authors presented Multiple Intelligence Learner-Centered Teaching (MILCT) and enumerated some techniques for active classroom management and better learning. This is, not only to create interest among students on a particular topic but ultimately allow the teachers to reach out to students who may learn more optimally in different ways. *'Impart knowledge in a way a student can easily understand and learn'*. I wish the higher education authorities heed this call in the near future.

The important role of culture in contributing to the etiology, maintenance, and treatment of disease has become increasingly clear. Although our goals of prevention and treatment of disease and maintenance of health may be the same across cultures, cultures vary in their definitions of what is considered "healthy" or "mature" (Tseng & McDermott, 1981). Cultural differences also exist in perceptions of problems and in preferred strategies for coping with them (Terrell, 1992). Cultural beliefs and practices influence concept of sickness as well as treatment modalities, both the therapist's as well as the client's definitions and understandings of the problem need to be taken into consideration for quality health. Western approaches to treatment of abnormal behavior may prove insensitive or inappropriate when applied across cultures. This book examines how cultural religious factors influence health and disease processes, and the need for indigenous culture-specific approaches to treat them in Ethiopia.

There is a belief among majority of Ethiopian people that health is a 'gift of God' and evil forces can cause sickness. Sickness can be caused by forces of witchcraft, evil eye and other believed negative forces and then the remedy is believed to be magicoreligious practices like Holy water, traditional healing by *debteras* and other delusive healers. The indigenous traditional healing practices can continue to be useful for communitarian values and curing different health issues for the Ethiopian people as long as the healer and healee hold similar worldview. A closer look at these traditional indigenous healing practices and scholarly discussions can increase the desire for better understanding and acceptance of local indigenous cultures as against the Western doctrines and therapeutic models. Further, it can also inspire scholars to create frameworks on culture-specific education and therapeutic interventions in Ethiopia.

It is not only psychology but education as a whole needs to be culture-sensitive and culture-specific. Ethiopia needs to develop her own theories, concepts and behavioral terms that can best describe human dynamism efficiently rather than wasting the precious time in adapting culturally incompatible philosophies of the dominant western culture.

This book recommends a significant shift in the discipline of psychology and education, which is dominated by western thinking, towards more culture-specific approach giving due considerations for the local culture, customs and praxis of different societies in Ethiopia. The authors wish that the readers who are interested in culture-sensitive psychology and education will benefit from this volume as it is written in a straightforward, jargon-free style that is accessible to the educated, layperson and students of social science and public health. It would serve very well as a supplemental text in many areas within psychology, in social science theory and methodology, cultural studies, social policy, and philosophy.

Bibliography

1. Abbink, J.(1996). "The Challenge of Education in Ethiopian Agro-Pastoral Societies. Surma Childhood in Crisis." In (Ed.) Habtamu Wondimu Research Papers on the situation of children and adolescentsin Ethiopia. Proceedings pp 115-136.
2. Abraham H. (1996). "Child-rearing practices in Siltigna-speaking community: Impact on the Development ofIndependence and Social Responsibility." In (ed) Habtamu Wondimu Research papers on the situation of children and adolescents in Ethiopia.
3. Adams, C. (2007). From Warrior to Magician: Entering the Realm of the Miraculous, Retrieved from http://www.spiritofmaat.com
4. Alkebulan, A. A. (2007) Defending the Paradigm Journal of Black Studies, Vol. 37, No. 3, 410-427.
5. Asante, M. K. (1987). The Afrocentric idea. Philadelphia: Temple University Press.
6. Asante, M. K. (1995). Afrocentricity: The theory of social change. Retrieved from http://www.africawithin.com/asante/social_change.htm.
7. Baker, S. B. (2000). School counselling for the twenty-first century. NY: Prentice Hall.
8. Banks, J. A. (1997). Educating Citizens in a Multicultural Society. NY: Teachers College Press.
9. Battell, D. C. (2005). The Ethiopian Orthodox Church and its Monastic Tradition. Retrieved on December 21, 2005 from WHO.
10. Berscheid, E, and Reis, (1998). Attraction and close relationship (1st ed.) New York: MC-Grew hill company.
11. Berz, Joan; Flanagan, Laura A. (2008). Inside Out and Outside In: Psychodynamic Clinical Theory and Psychopathology in Contemporary Multicutural Contexts. New York: Jason Aronson. pp. 229–242.

12. Block & Dworking, G. (1976). The IQ Controversy. New York, Pantheon Books.

13. Bloland, P. A. (1992). Qualitative research in student affairs. Los Angeles, CA: University of California at Los Angeles.

14. Bogdan, R. C., & Biklen, S. K. (1992). Qualitative research for education: An introduction to theory and method. Boston: Allyn and Bacon.

15. Borders, L. D. & Drury, S. M. (1992). Comprehensive school counselling programs: A review for policymakers and practitioners. Journal of Counselling and Development, 70, 487-498.

16. Braud. W. & Anderson. R. (1998). Transpersonal research methods for the social sciences. New Delhi: Sage Publications.

17. Brewi, J, and Brennan, A. (1989). Celebrate midlife: Jungian archetypes and mid life spirituality (1st ed.) New York: USA.

18. Bruner, J. (1990). Acts of meaning. Cambridge: Harvard University Press.

19. Campbell, C. A., & Dahir, C. A. (1997). Sharing the vision: The national standards for school counselling programs. Alexandria, VA: American School Counsellor Association.

20. Carroll, L. and Dyckman (1986). Chaos or creation: spirituality in mid life,(1sted.) New York: Paulist press.

21. Castillo, R. J. (1997). Cultural assessment. "In" R. J. Castillo, Culture and mental illness (pp. 55-75). Pacific Grove, CA: Brooks/Cole.

22. Central Statistical Authority and ORC Macro Ethiopia Demographic and Health Survey 2000. Addis Ababa Ethiopia and Calverton, Maryland, USA,

23. Chapman, A. (2006). Howard Gardner's Multiple Intelligences. Retrieved on 23 April 2006 from www.businessballs.com.

24. Chislett & Chapman, (2005). Free Multiple Intelligence Test. Retrieved from www.businessballs.com.

25. Claver, F. (1995). The social marginalization of tribal peoples and their contribution to ecological health. A report delivered in a conference on the concerns of indigenous peoples, Hua Hin, Thailand.

26. Cole, M. (1996). Cultural psychology: A once and future discipline. Cambridge, MA: Harvard.

27. Collen, R. (1996). Men, midlife, and mysticism Retrieved from http://www.sonic.net.

28. Conwey, J. (1997). Men in midlife crisis,(1sted.) New York: charier victor pub.

29. Cooper CR., Denner J. (1998). Theories linking culture and psychology: Universal and Community-Specific Processes. Annual Review of Psychology. 49:559-84.

30. Cory, T. (2003). Brainstorming: Techniques for New Ideas. Minnesota: iUniverse Pub.

31. Daniels, M. (1997). Holism, integration & the transpersonal. Transpersonal Psychology Review, 1(3), 12-16.

32. Daniels, M. (1998). Transpersonal psychology and the paranormal. Transpersonal Psychology Review, 2(3), 17-31.

33. David H.olson and John DeFrain (1997). Marriage and family (3rd ed.) London: Mayfield Company.

34. DuBois, Cora (1960). The People of Alor : a social-psychological study of an East Indian Island, Cambridge : Harvard University Press.

35. Eaton, W.O., & Ritchot, K.F.M (1995). Physical maturation and information processing speed in childhood. Developmental psychology, 31, 967 - 972.

36. Engels, D. W., & Dameron, J. D. (Eds.). (1990). The professional counsellor: Competencies, performance guidelines, and assessment (2nd ed.). Alexandria, VA: American Counselling Association.

37. Eric Shiraev and David Levg. (2004). Introduction to cross cultural psychology, (2nd ed.) USA: Pearson Education Inc.

38. Erikson, E. (l968). Identity: Youth in crisis, New York: Norton.

39. Federal Democratic Republic of Ethiopia Ministry of Health. Health and Health Related Indicators 2003/04. Addis Ababa, December 2004.

40. Ferguson, R. (1998). Can schools narrow the Black-White test score gap? In C. Jencks & M. Phillips (Eds.), The Black-White test score gap (pp. 318-374). Washington, DC: The Brookings Institution.

41. Fisher S., Greenberg R. P. (1977). "The Scientific Credibility of Freud's Theories and Therapy", New York: Basic Books.

42. Fisher, Helen (1983). The Sex Contract – the Evolution of Human Behavior, William Morrow & Co

43. Freire, P. (1972). Pedagogy of the oppressed. Ringwood, Australia: Penguin.

44. Freud, S. (1928). The future of an illusion. London: Hogarth Press.

45. Frie, R. (2003). (Ed.) Understanding experience. New York: Routledge.

46. Fry, C.L. (1999). Anthropological theories of age and aging. In V.L. Bengtson & K.W. Schaie (Eds.), handbook of theories of aging. New York: Springer.

47. Gardner, H. (1983). Frames of Mind. New York: Basic Book Inc.

48. Gardner, H. (1999). Intelligence Reframed: Multiple Intelligences for the 21st Century, New York, Basic Book Inc.

49. Gardner, H. (2003). Multiple Intelligences After Twenty Years. Paper presented at the American Educational Research Association, Chicago.

50. Gemechu, B. & Assefa, T. (2006). Marriage Practices

Among The Gidda Oromo, Northern Wollega, Ethiopia:Nordic Journal of African Studies 15(3): 240–255.

51. Ginter, E. J., Scalise, J. J., & Presse, N. (1990). The elementary school counselor's role: Perceptions of teachers. The School Counselor, 38(1), 19-23

52. Goldhaber, D., & Brewer, D. (1997). Evaluating the effect of teacher degree level on educational performance. In W. Fowler (Ed.), Developments in school finance, 1996 (pp. 197-210). Washington.

53. Goleman, D. (1995). Emotional intelligence. New York: Bantam Books.

54. Goodenough, W. H. (1996). "Culture" - Encyclopedia of Cultural Anthropology.

55. Gorden, R. L. (1969). Interviewing: Strategy, Techniques and Tactics Homewood Ill, Dorsey Press.

56. Gottfredson, L. (1998). The General Intelligence Factor. Scientific American 9,4, (Winter, 1998): 24-29.

57. Gould, S. J., (1996). The Mismeasure of Man, W. W. Norton & Company.

58. Greenwald, R., Hedges, L., & Laine, R. (1996). The effect of school resources on student achievement. Review of Educational Research, 66(3), 361-396.

59. Gudykunst, W. B. (1997). Cultural variability in communication. Communication Research, 24 (4): 327-348.

60. Gysbers, N. C. & Henderson, P. (1988). Developing and managing your school guidance program. Alexandria, VA: American Association for Counselling and Development.

61. Hanushek, E. (1986). The economics of schooling: Production and efficiency in public schools. Journal of Economic Literature, 24(3), 1141-78.

62. Hanushek, E., Kain, J., & Rivkin, S. (1999). Do higher salaries buy better teachers? Working Paper No. 7082. Cambridge: National Bureau of Economic Research.

63. HarlockElizabeth, B (1981) Developmental psychology, (5th ed.) India: Tata McGraw-Hill publishing company.

64. Hawi, H. O. (2005). A search for an alternative Afro-centric development theory. Retrieved from http://www.codesria.org.

65. Headland, T. N. Pike K. L., & Harris M. (1990). (Ed.). "Emics" and "Etics": The insider/outsider debate. London: Sage Publications.

66. Heidegger, M. (1962). Being and time. Oxford, Basil Blackwell.

67. Henderson, L. (1996). Instructional design of interactive multimedia: A cultural critique. Educational Technology Research and Development, 44(4), 85-104.

68. Hendricks, G., & Weinhold, B. (1982). Transpersonal approaches to counselling and psychotherapy. London: Love Publishing Company.

69. Heppner, P. P., Kivlighan, D. M., & Wampold, B. E. (1992). Research design in counselling. Pacific Grove, CA: Brooks/Cole.

70. Herrnstein, R., & Murray, C. (1994). The Bell Curve: Intelligence and Class Structure in American life. New York: Free Press.

71. Hillocks, G. (1995). Teaching Writing as Reflective Practice. N Y: Teachers College Press.

72. Husserl, E. (1970). Logical investigations New York, Humanities Press

73. Impara, J. C, & Plake, B. S. (1995). Comparing counsellors', school administrators', and teachers' knowledge in student assessment. Measurement and Evaluation in Counselling and Development, 28, 78-87.

74. International Encyclopedia of the Social Sciences.(1977). 11th ed., Vol. 10, New York, The Macimillan Company and the Free Press.

75. James, W. (1936). The varieties of religious experience. NY: Modern Library.

76. Janetius, T. (2003). The emerging worldview of Cordillera indigenous peoples of selected provinces: implications for psychotherapy. Unpublished Doctoral Dissertation. De La Salle University, Manila, Philippines.

77. Janetius, T. (2005). Buddha Brainstorming (BBs) Technique. Retrieved on April 25, 2008 from http://janetius.page.tl/Buddha-Brainstorming.htm.

78. Janetius. T. & Mulat. A. (2006). Multiple Intelligence Learner-Centered Teaching : a new paradigm for college education in Ethiopia, Proceedings of the conference on Teacher education for Sustainable Development in Ethiopia, Debre Zeit, May 5-6, 2006.

79. Janetius, T. (2007). Far From Freud: Difficulty in Explaining Psychosexual Development in Ethiopia, Retrieved from http://janetius.page.tl/Far-From-Freud.htm

80. Janetius, T., Mulat, A., & Mini. T. C. (2007). Culture-Sensitive College Teaching in Ethiopia: A Conceptual Model. A Paper presented at the First Annual Research Conference on Education for Sustainable Development in Ethiopia: Opportunities and Challenges, Alpha University College, Addis Ababa

81. John W.Santrock (1997). Psychology (6th ed.) India: tata McGraw- Hill Company.

82. Jules and Henry. (1998). Culture against men, (1st ed.) Canada: Random house of Canada publishing company.

83. Jung C.G (1933). Modern man in search of soul(1ST ed.) New York: Harvest Books.

84. Jung C.G (1954). Psychology of transference (1st ed.) New York: Pantheon Books.

85. Jung C.G. (1969). The stages of life-collected works Vol.8 (R.F.C. Hull, Trans) New Jersey: Princeton university Press.

86. Jung, C. G. (1958). The collected works of C. G. Jung (vol. II). Princeton, NJ: Princeton University Press.

87. Jung, C. G. (1989). Memories, dreams, reflections. Vancouver: Vintage Books.

88. Kearney, R. (1984). Dialogues with contemporary continental thinkers. Manchester: Manchester University Press.

89. Kail, R. (1991). Developmental change in speed of processing during childhood and adolescence. Psychological bulletin, 109, 490 – 501.

90. Komarek, K. (2003). Universal primary education in multilingual societies: Supporting its implementation in Sub-Saharan Africa and beyond. Cited in Mekonnen, A. G. Y. (2006). Pride in foreign Language, and prejudice in indigenous languages. Proceedings of the conference on teacher education for sustainable development in Ethiopia, Addis Ababa University.

91. Kothari, C. R. (1989). Research Methodology- Methods and Techniques. Delhi: Wishwa Prakashan.

92. Krechevsky, M., & Seidel, S. (1998). Minds at work: Applying multiple intelligences in the classroom. In R. Sternberg & W. Williams (Eds.), Intelligence, instruction, and assessment. Mahwah, NJ: Lawrence Erlbaum.

93. Krippner, S. (1988). Shamans: The first healers. In G. Doore (Ed.), Shaman's path: Healing, personal growth and empowerment (pp. 101-114). Boston, MA: Shambala Publications.

94. Ladson, G & Billings (1995). Toward a Theory of Culturally Relevant Pedagogy, American Educational Research Journal, Vol. 32, No. 3 (Autumn, 1995), pp. 465-491.

95. Lajoie, D. H., & Shapiro, S. I. (1992). Definitions of transpersonal psychology: The first twenty-three years. Journal of Transpersonal Psychology, 24(1), 79-98.

96. Landis, J.T.(1966). Personal adjustment, marriage and family (1st ed.) N J: Prentice Hall Inc.

97. Lapuz, L.V (1986). Filipino marriage in crisis (1st ed.) Quezon City: New Day Publishers.

98. Lasswell, M.E and Lasswell, T.E (1982). Marriage and the family (1st ed) Washington DC: Heath and Company.

99. Leach, P. (1997). Your baby and child: From birth to age five. 5th edition. New York: Knopf.

100. Lefkowitz, M.R. (1996). "Not Out of Africa: How" Afrocentrism" Became an Excuse to Teach Myth as History". NY: Basic Books.

101. Levinson, D.J. (1978). The seasons of a man's life(1st ed.) Naugatuck: Knopf.

102. Linstone, H. & Turloff, M. (1975). The Delphi method: Techniques and applications. London: Addison- Wesley.

103. Long, T. E. and Jeffrey K. H. 1985. A Reconception of Socialization. Sociological Theory 3(1):39-49.

104. McAdoo, H. P. (1993). Ethnic families: Strengths that are found in diversity. "In" McAdoo (Ed.), Family ethnicity: Strength in diversity (pp. 3-14). CA: Sage Publications.

105. McClanaghan, M. E. (2000). A strategy for helping students learn how to learn. Education, 120, 479-486.

106. Mead, M. (1949). Coming of Age in Samoa. A Mentor Book) Mass Market Paperback.

107. Measor, L. (1985). "Interviewing: a Strategy in Qualitative Research" in R Burgess (ed) Strategies of Educational Research: Qualitative Methods. Lewes: Falmer Press.

108. Mekonnen, A. G. Y. (2006). Pride in foreign Language, and prejudice in indigenous languages: A paper presented at the conference on teacher education for sustainable development in Ethiopia, Addis Ababa University.

109. Mendoza, R. H. (1989). An empirical scale to measure type and degree of acculturation in Mexican-American

adolescents and adults. Journal of Cross-Cultural Psychology, 20(4), 372-385.

110. Merleau-Ponty, M. (1979). Phenomenology of perception. The humanities press. N.J.

111. Mills. J. (1999). In search of a method: New directions in philosophical counselling. Paper presented at Canadian Society for Philosophical Practice, Ontario Philosophical Association, Guelph, Ontario.

112. Mkabela, Q. (2005). Using the Afrocentric Method in Researching Indigenous African Culture, The Qualitative Report Volume 10 Number 1 March 2005 178-189.

113. Mohanty, C. T. (1997). Under Western Eyes: Feminist Scholarship and Colonial Discourses, in Chandra Mohanty et al. (eds): Third World Women and the Politics of Feminism, Indiana Uni. Press.

114. Monk, D., & King-Rice, J. (1994). Multi-level teacher resource effects on pupil performance in secondary mathematics and science: The role of teacher subject matter preparation. In R. Ehrenberg (Ed.), Choices and consequences: Contemporary policy issues in education (pp. 29-58). Ithaca, NY: ILR Press.

115. Mpofu, E. (2002). Indigenization of the psychology of human intelligence in Sub-Saharan Africa. In W. J. Lonner, D. L. Dinnel, S. A. Hayes, & D. N. Sattler (Eds.), Online Readings in Psychology and Culture (Unit 5, Chapter 2), Center for Cross-Cultural Research, Western Washington University.

116. Murphy, M. D. (2007). Culture and Personality, Retrieved from http://anthropology.ua.edu.

117. Myre, Sim (1974). "Guide to Psychiatry, 3rd edition" Churchill Livingstone, Edinburgh and London, ISBN 0 443 01161 3. page 35, page 407.

118. National Center for Health Statistics. (2000a). centers for

diseases control and prevention growth charts. Retrieved from www.nap.edu/openbook/030907177/html/3.html.

119. NCTPE (1998). Baseline survey on Harmful traditional practices in Ethiopia, Addis.

120. Neugarten, B.L., Moore, J.W., & Lowe, J. C. (1965). Age norms, age constraints, and adult socialization. American journal of sociology,70, 710 – 717.

121. Oakley, A. (1981). "Interviewing women: a contradiction in terms" in H Roberts (ed) Doing Feminist Research. London, Routledge & Kegan Paul.

122. Owen, R. I. (1989). The application of some ideas from anthroplogy to counselling, therapy and cross-cultural counselling. British Association for Counselling and the American Association for Counselling Development. Uxbridge: Uxbridge University.

123. Palermo, J. (1997). Reading Asante's Myth of Afrocentricity: An Ideological Critique, Buffalo State College. Retrieved from http://www.ed.uiuc.edu/eps/PES-Yearbook/97_docs/palermo.html.

124. Panos, P. T., & Panos, A. J. (2000). A model for a culture-sensitive assessment of patients in health care settings. Social Work in Health Care, 31(1), 49-62.

125. Papoutsaki, E. (2006). De-westernising Research Methodologies: Alternative Approaches to Research for Higher Education Curricula in Developing Countries, Global Colloquium of the UNESO Forum on Higher Education, Research & Knowledge, Paris.

126. Pelto, P. J., & Pelto. G. H. (1978). Units of observation: "Emic" and "Etic" approaches. "In" Anthropological research: The structure of inquiry. Cambridge University Press.

127. Phinney, J., & Landin, J. (1998). Research paradigms for studying ethnic minority families within and across

groups. In V. McLoyd & L. Steinberg (Eds.), Research on minority adolescents: Conceptual, methodological, and theoretical issues, Hillsdale, NJ: Lawrence Erlbaum.

128. Plummer, K. (1983). Documents of Life: an introduction to the problems and literature of a humanistic method. London, Unwin Hyman.

129. Prah, K. K. (2003). Going Native: Language of instruction for education, development and African emancipation. Cited in Mekonnen, A. G. Y. (2006). Pride in foreign Language, and prejudice in indigenous languages: Achievement implications of the use of English versus mother tongues in Ethiopia. Proceedings of the conference on teacher education for sustainable development in Ethiopia, College of Education, Addis Ababa University.

130. Reber, A. S. (1995). The Penguin Dictionary of Psychology, 2nd ed. Toronto: Penguin Books.

131. Richards, P. S. & Bergin, A. E. (1997). A Spiritual strategy for counselling and psychotherapy. Washington, D.C.: American Psychological Association.

132. Ridley, C. & Lingle, D. (1993). Cultural empathy in multicultural counselling: A multidimensional process model, In P. Pederson, J. Draguns, W. Lonner, & J. Trible's, (editors). Counselling across cultures, 4th Edition, Thousand Oaks, CA: Sage.

133. Rogers, C.R. (1951). Client-centred therapy. Boston: Houghton Mifflin.

134. Sampson, J. P., Jr., Vacc, N. A., & Loesch, L. C. (1998). The practice of career counselling by specialists & counselors in general practice. The Career Development Quarterly, 46, 404-415.

135. Santos, D. (1998). Multicultural perspective in three international schools in the Philippines. "In" Bernado, (Ed.), Understanding behavior bridging cultures (pp 159 - 166).

Manila: De La Salle University Press.

136. Sayre, N.E. & Gallagher, J. D. (2001). The young child and the environment. Allyn & Bacon.

137. Sears, S. J. (1991). The scope of practice of the secondary level school counselor. Retrieved from http://www.ericdigests.org/pre-9219/scope.htm

138. Segall, M. H., Dasen, P. R., Berry, J. W., & Poortinga, Y. H. (1999). Human Behavior in Global Perspective: An Introduction to Cross-Cultural Psychology (2nd Ed.). Boston: Allyn and Bacon, pp.399.

139. Semali, L. (1999). "Community as a Classroom: Dilemmas of Valuing African Indigenous Literacy in Education" in International Review of Education, 45 (3-4), 305-319.

140. Shertzer, B., & Stone, S. C. (1981). Fundamentals of guidance (4th ed.). Boston: Houghton-Mifflin.

141. Silva, R. (2001). What is transpersonal psychology? Retrieved from http://www.cyberpsychologist.com/FAQ.htm#Transperso nal%20Psychology

142. Sinha, D. (1997). Indigenising psychology. In J. W. Berry, Y. H. Poortinga, & J. Pandey (Eds.), Handbook of Cross-cultural Psychology, Vol 1. (pp.129-169). Needham Heights, MA: Allyn & Bacon.

143. Smith, M. K. (2002). 'Howard Gardner and multiple intelligences', the encyclopedia of informal education, Retrieved from www.infed.org.

144. Smith, M. L., & Glass, G. V. (1987). Research and evaluation in education and the social sciences. Englewood Cliffs, NJ: Pr.-Hall.

145. Spiegelberg, H. (1970). Phenomenology, in: Encyclopaedia Britannica, vol. 17 (14th ed), pp. 810-812.

146. Strauss, A. & Corbin, J. (1990). Basics of qualitative research: Grounded theory procedures and techniques.

Newbury Park, CA: Sage Publications.

147. Strauss, R., & Vogt, W. (2001). It's what you know, not how you learned to teach it: Evidence from a study of the effects of knowledge and pedagogy on student achievement. Paper presented at the annual meeting of American Educational Finance Association, Cincinnati Weishen & Peng, 1993.

148. Su, J. (2006). Culture and theory, Class notes on Introduction to cultural Psychology, University of Minnesota. Retrieved from http://www.psych.umn.edu.

149. Sue, D.W. & Sue, D. (1990). Counselling the culturally different, New York: John Wile

150. Tedla, E. (1995). Sankofa: African Thought and Education. NY: Peter Lang.

151. Trimble, J. E. (2000). Considering the cultures within. Retrieved from www.radcliffe.edu/quarterly/200004/hidden-6.html.

152. Tymofievich, M., & Leroux, J. A. (2000). Counsellors' competencies using assessments. Measurement & Evaluation in Counselling and Development, 33, 50-59.

153. United Nations Declaration on the Rights of Indigenous Peoples (2007) Retrieved from www.iwgia.org/sw248.asp.

154. Van Galen, G.P.(1993). Handwriting: A developmental perspective. In Kkaverboer, B. Hopkins, & R.H. Guez (Eds.), Motor development in early and later childhood: Longitudinal approaches. Cambridge university press.

155. Walker, C. E. (2000). We Can't Go Home Again: An Argument about Afrocentrism. Oxford University.

156. Walsh, R., & Vaughan, F. (Eds.). (1993). Paths beyond ego: The transpersonal vision. LA: Tarcher-Putnam.

157. Wachs, T.D. (2000). Necessary but not sufficient: the respective roles of single and multiple influences on individual development. Washington, DC: American

Psychological Association.

158. Weimer, M. G. (2002). Learner-centered teaching: Five key changes to practice. San Francisco: Jossey-Bass.

159. Wiersma, W. (1995). Research methods in education (6th ed.). Boston, MA: Allyn & Bacon.

160. Wilber, K. (1983). A sociable god: Toward a new understanding of religion. London: Shambhala.

161. Wilber, K. (2000). Sex, ecology, spirituality: The spirit of evolution (2nd rev. ed.). Boston: Shambhala.

162. Yan, J.H., Thomas, J.R., & Stelmach, G.E., & Thomas K.T. (2000). Developmental features of rapid aiming arm movments across the lifespan. Journal of motor behaviour, 32, 121 – 140

163. Yeo, A. (2000). Counselling trends in postmodernist thinking in counselling. "In" Clemeña (Ed.), Counselling in Asia (pp. 6-19). Manila: De La Salle University Press.

About the Authors

Dr Janetius is an Indian Psychologist and an ardent qualitative researcher graduated from De La Salle University, Philippines. His doctoral research was on '*The emerging worldview and health practices of Cordillera indigenous people in the Philippines*'. He was a teaching faculty of Psychology, University of Gondar, Ethiopia. Currently he is the Director of Centre for Counselling and Guidance, Sree Saraswathi Thyagaraja College, Pollachi, India; also heads a newly formed Psychology Department.

Dr Mini, T.C. is a graduate of International Institute of Population Studies, Mumbai. She holds a Doctorate in Statistics from Andhra University, India and currently working as the Chief Academic Officer of Cheran Group of Educational Institutions, South India. She worked for four years in the College of Medicine and Health Sciences, Gondar, Ethiopia. She is a recipient of a major project (2010-2012) from the Indian Council of Social Science Research for studying the '*Health and worldview of Malayarayan Tribal Community in the Western Ghats*'.

Alemayehu Tibebe is a graduate in Applied Psychology from University of Gondar and holds a Masters in Public Health from Mekelle University. Currently he is working as the Executive Director for Tigrai Private Health Facilities Association. Earlier to that he worked as a lecturer at Military Staff College in Ethiopia and also was part of college counseling services to support military personnel and their families. He has conducted many researches in psycho-social and cultural factors relating to culture-specific psychology.

Notes...

Notes...

_____

www.ingramcontent.com/pod-product-compliance
Lightning Source LLC
Chambersburg PA
CBHW050443290526
45786CB00006B/2139